P9-DEY-503

# PRIMITIVES

## Our American Heritage

### Second Series

**Kathryn McNerney**

**COLLECTOR BOOKS**

*A Division of Schroeder Publishing Co., Inc.*

The current values in this book should be used only as a guide. They are not intended to set prices, which vary from one section of the country to another. Auction prices as well as dealer prices vary greatly and are affected by condition as well as demand. Neither the Author nor the Publisher assumes responsibility for any losses that might be incurred as a result of consulting this guide.

Additional copies of this book may be ordered from:

Collector Books
P.O. Box 3009
Paducah, KY 42001

@$14.95 Add $1.00 for postage and handling.

Copyright: Kathryn McNerney, 1987

This book or any part thereof may not be reproduced without the written consent of the Author and Publisher.

*For My Children:*
*Sharon – Tom L. – Molly*

# Appreciation

Along with new contributors to BOOK II remain those who also offered material for BOOK I. To each . . . named and unnamed . . . I am intensely grateful. Thank you.

Exhibitors, Dealers, Promoters at Florida Sunshine, Norma King Antiques and Hoosier Antiques Exposition Shows; Malls at Bayard Country Store, Orange Park Antiques and The Loft in Florida; Lewiston Landing in New York; Antiques Unlimited and Murfreesboro Antiques in Tennessee; Restorations at Indiana's Spring Mill Park, The Homeplace 1850 at The Land Between the Lakes, and Old Fort Niagara Association in New York. Clark's Corner, Dennis Sullivan, the Blincoes, For My Daughter's Antiques, Joan Ekola, John Noven, Judy Lee, Lorene and Robert Rodgers, Mrs. Hamilton, the Klingensmiths and Jim Robertsons, Timely Treasures and Zelma Neale in Florida; Helen Berline, Idaho; Cliff Buckalew and Lela Neptune in Indiana; Concord Antiques, Kentucky; Shoppe of Antiquity, Michigan; Stimson & Associates International, New York; Marie Norris, Tennessee; Carleton Cobb, Virginia; Bellaire Galleries, Wisconsin.

# Contents

# Introduction

BOOK I introduced homesteading, illustrating, describing and evaluating hundreds of primitives by which our pioneers were able to meet and learn to live in partnership with the American wilderness.

BOOK II continues with many more subjects, progressing to include articles acquired when family interests and holdings expanded, building the future of our country itself . . . primitives growing up.

Importantly, in our step by step heritage are those pieces regarded as "Country Collectibles". The previously-restrictive Primitives umbrella began unfurling to cover endless articles relating to maturing regions, exact interpretation of differences between the two category headings never specifically defined . . . seemingly not expected . . . just matter of factly accepted in our modern tempo. This may have happened when "Country Cousins" were fairly plentiful and Primitives were often hard to find. Further, all share a mutual lack of sophistication in intent and materials. They usually combine well with each other and with dissimilar types of artifacts, functionally and decoratively.

Too, there should be heritage "antiques" for oncoming generations to purchase, enjoy and feel (like the one-of-a-kind marvelous patina of woods only age and usage can properly bestow), tangible evidences of how their forefathers lived and labored, putting into each object they made a little bit of themselves. Best of all, most folks are comfortable with them . . . their hominess.

Other than necessities and anxiously-crafted gifts made in the American wilderness are the pieces brought here by immigrants, that were shipped as an inheritance or even purchased as families prospered. Finally after a long period of time, they are now considered, if so thought of at all in that regard, as "native" as the families consider themselves.

And as a rose is a rose is a rose . . . no two identical . . . so is this true herein. Similar types in BOOK I and BOOK II are LOOK ALIKES . . . with natural individual differences . . . typically ambitious American efforts to improve existing circumstances and create beyond survival a little comfort and/or beauty in a stark environment.

NOTE: Everything is considered PREMIUM (mint, near-mint, excellent) unless mentioned in concurrence with owners. Measurements may slightly vary.

CORNCRIB. Homesteaders commonly cleared trees from their land to raise cabins and out-buildings (as shown at The Homeplace 1850). Corner-locking insured against this shed being blown over in gale force winds. Logs were cut and shaped, the mortise being the cavity into which the tenon was first properly cut and shaped to fit, called "mortise and tenon joints".

CORNSHELLER. ca: early 1800s smithy made; original red on two thick planks, one convex, the other concave with a handle, both with shaped ends where a wooden pin (later heavy wire replacement) through matching holes held the wood together; headless square nails became the graters. The lower board fastened to an easel-like stand, the handle half pulled back and forth over an ear of corn placed between the nail stubs shucked kernels from the cob, dropping them into a tub beneath; 12"L x 8"W. (Rare).

WOOD MEASURES. All bent-wood; New England origin. Center 8″ dia. has a twice-wrapped-around wood top band; impressed "W. SWEET" on outside of rim and "B.TIDD" is cut into the bottom; 4″H.

Next size 6¾″ dia. is two-banded iron and iron-braced crisscrosses on the bottom; 4¾″H; impressed on interior bottom: "Made For KIRKHOLDER & RAUSCH CO. BY E. B. FRYE & SON WILTON N.H.".

Smallest 5¾″ dia.; 3½″H; has inside base impressed: "MADE BY E. B. FRYE & SON WILTON N.H.," and printed on outside "DRY 1 QT. MEASURE"; two narrow iron bands.

GRAIN MEASURE. Six initials cut into wrapped rim band; double nail rows holding wrapped wood; New England origin.

MEASURES. ca: 1800s. Sturdy; larger ones for grains, tobacco and such while smaller sizes were often meal measures. They came in many sizes, usually round with a few rarer squares, various woods, some iron bound; for innumberable usages.

GRAIN MEASURE. ca: 1800s. Factory-made of wood with iron bands; 12″ dia. about 8″H; used for grains, herbs, butter, sugar, cheeses and more.

GRAIN MEASURE. ca: 1850-1860. Steamed and wrapped oak; strongly-looped-over separate rim band; penknife-carved "B. TIDD" on inside bottom, a popular way of marking maker and/or owner.

Homemade in the 1800s for use by owner's family as a SEED GRAINS SCRAPER. Found in a long-boarded-up shed on their farm. Points are still sharp.

SEEDCORN DRYERS. Ears impaled on sharp points; filled racks were then hung high in warm barn lofts or home attics where drying kernels awaited spring test plantings.

STEELYARDS (STILYERDS) (PEA SCALE). ca: latter 1700s. Uncommon squared-weight in iron; three hooks, one to hold or hang, two for objects to be weighed.

WORKING GRIST MILL. Established 1817; southern Indiana Spring Mill Museum; various sized iron WHEELS used; iron, wood and brass PLATFORM SCALE complete with weights, (comparable one for sale would be about $250.00). Settlers toted their corn to the Mill to be crushed or ground into meal; some walked, others rode mules, a few rode horseback. Millers commonly kept a TOLL MEASURE, a little larger than a peck, of meal as payment for their services.

BUHR (GRINDING) STONE. ca: early 1800s. Massive; center has various-sized parts to allow use on separate axle dimensions; a smithy has added the wide iron band; seen at an Indiana museum, but a comparable one, considering age, rarity, weight and condition would be very expensive.

MEAL SCOOP (PALETTE). Hand-whittled, finger and thumb holes; used in an Illinois grist mill to scoop meal, flour and grains from bins into sacks.

GRISTMILL HAND GRINDER. ca: 1817. Seen at an Indiana museum; hand turned; wood with iron fixtures; for small amounts of meal; grain was put in the mouth of the box, dropped through for grinding or cracking, and came out the trap door. Not for sale but a comparable one would be valued at several hundred dollars.

GRAIN SHOVEL. Handcut light wood with curved handle; about 50"L.

GRAIN SCOOP. ca: 1700s. From New England, handcut of one piece pine with half rim at back in varying widths; used at a grist mill; hanging eye penetrates side to side.

GRAINS SCRAPER (PULLER). ca: 1800s. Used at a northern granary, this type also might be found on a farm; hand-whittled from hardwood; 16"L x 6"W.

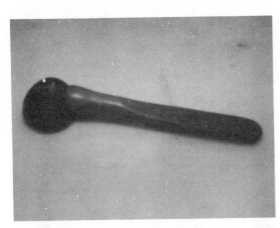

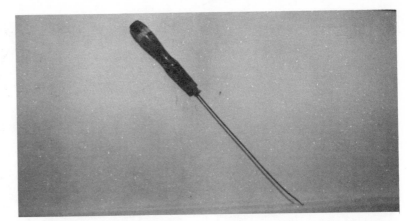

SEED MEASURE. Wood, marked: "Property of A. Cornell Seed Co., Mo. U.S.A."; 5¾"L overall; ball end 1"W x ½"D.

TOWSACK NEEDLE. Large-eyed blunt needle similar to a bodkin (handgrip at other end) that could punch holes, pull through heavy twine , sewing up sacks made from tow (broken and coarse parts of flax and hemp woven into tough cloth); this might have also picked-out stitches when sack material was vital for frontier clothing and bedding; 7"L.

SIGN. ca: 1800s. THE HAYNES GIN CO. (with list of services provided) was long in operation at Cannonsburgh, Tennessee (now called Murfreesboro). The gin removed seeds from cotton, an essential operation to the planters in marketing their field crops. These original building signs are difficult to find and would be valued for purchase at a minimum of $350.00 depending upon information on them. The BALE of GIN-NED COTTON seen at a display has had mice-browsers. Toy cotton wagon on top.

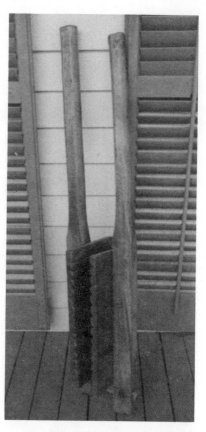

LARD SQUEEZER. Hardwood; grooved wide pincers brought together with handle pressure squeezed fat from pork bits floating to the top from meat being cooked in kettles; 49½"L x 27½"W grooves.

HOGHOUSE (PIGHOUSE) and adjoining HOGPEN (PIGPEN). ca: 1840. Built of wood cut in clearing a Western Kentucky homestead, it both sheltered and restricted movements of domestic swine, whose food consisted of available nuts (preferably beech if any were about), chaff left over from mill grindings as pig feed filler, and slop (pigs not being notoriously fastidious eaters). Called "slopping the hogs", fairly nutritive kitchen wastes (they adored potato peelings) mixed with water or excess liquids after churning were poured into hollowed out log troughs. Wild pigs and sometimes even farm porkers were turned loose in warmer months to fend for themselves in the woods, existing on acorns, rooting for grubs, etc.

SAUSAGE GUN. The largest transparent hog intestines were thoroughly washed and slipped over the sheetiron tubes' snouts; here a worn hard-maple flat-bottomed plunger (pestle) forced "seasoned" chopped or ground meats (most often pork) into the casing which, when filled, was tied into small or large links (sections) and hung to dry (cure); small wire hanging ring.

AXE HEAD. A North Carolina blacksmith left hammer marks on this chisel-edge iron with its wholly-American heavy poll, adding a 2¾″ band for increased durability. Smithies also made handles, cut to personal dimensions. As our first construction tool, the axe was imperative for the frontiersman to fell, cut and chop square logs into beams, even use as a weapon. (For many collectors, painting reduces value.).

AMERICAN GOOSEWING BROADAXE. ca: 1700s, early 1800s. Blacksmith-made in western Kentucky. Intended for a left-handed owner, it was swung from that side with both hands, squaring round logs into square beams. It has a forged-on iron band ½″W at center tapered to ¼″ at ends on that one side only, customarily added (more in steel) for extra endurance. There is no touchmark for this fine work. Accurately resembling the gracefulness of the bird's wing, the hickory handle, after so long a time, is probably a replacement, having been slashed in front of the poll with two iron strips inserted (rather than the more common wood pins) for strength and to avoid coming out due to shrinkage of the wood; handle 19¼″L, squared poll across the top 3″ x 1½″W; blade 10¼″L from it's point to the back edge; 5⅜″ widest part top of poll to bottom of cutting edge.

HITTING MAUL (BEETLE). ca: 1800s. Hickory (oak was also used for these); applied wherever great hitting strength was required, as the maul striking an iron or hardwood wedge to split logs; center may have been originally shallow-cut for better aiming. 34″H.

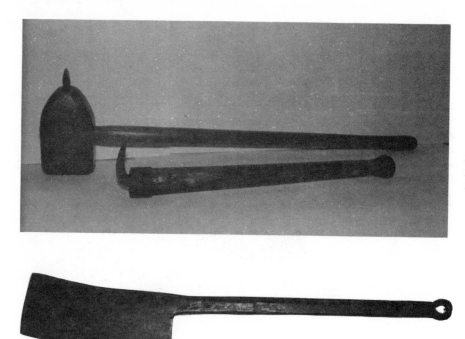

LOGGERS' PICKAROON. ca: early 1800s. Hand-fashioned; deep iron collar helps hold pick to wood handle; 19″L.

MALLET. ca: 1800s. Hickory; iron spur imbedded in mallet head; mallet 7½″L, 2½″D x 3½″W; handle 30¾″L.

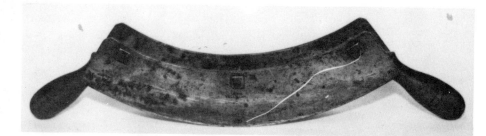

KNIFE FROW. ca: 1700s. Hand-fashioned of iron with long handle ending in hanging eye; sharp bottomside edge blade. (Rarity).

SILAGE CUTTER. Curved sharp lower edge iron blade; adjustable hardwood shaped and groove-trimmed handgrips, UP to chop, DOWN if idle; silage is fodder cut and stored in airtight silos (originally pits or vats) where compacting caused fermentation preservation for winter stock feeding. Machines now are generally replacements, although one of these handchoppers might still be used on smaller farms. (First invented in England about 1750, commercial "ensilage" choppers became extensively used in our American colonies on many large estates.).

WELL PLUG. ca: Early 1800s. Hand-cut hickory; leather banded.

BUCKET. ca: latter 1800s. Ranch Round-up CHUCKWAGON PAIL; heavy sheet tin, wood grip on squared bail (handle).

WELL BUCKET. ca: 1800s. Galvanized iron; heavy iron wire bail twisted to form loop for holding well rope; durable ears on each side.

LEATHER BUCKET. ca: 1880-1890. Both sides of handle and extra rim reinforcing are double sewn; held grains, water, etc. 9″ top dia. narrowing at base; 6″H.

WHEELBARROW WHEEL. Made by Pennsylvania Amish; iron-bound wood 21″ dia., axle 15″ across.

GRUBBING HOE. ca: 1792-1805. Found in Florida's N.E. coastal area where plantation blacksmiths commonly made such tools; from iron, it lacks its big round (wood) handle; these extra large iron collars are typical of the period, a help in determining age.

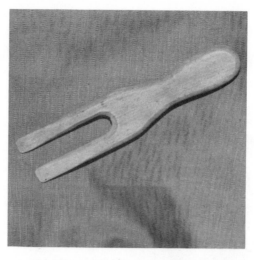

CABBAGE PLANTER. Indiana origin, hard maple; for stoopwork, hand-planting cabbage "sets" raised from seed in a frame (bed).

GIG. For fishing; made by a blacksmith from one piece of iron with four prongs, wood handle and brass ferrule.

BLUEGRASS SEED STRIPPER. All original with red stain, but manufacturer's black lettering too faint to accurately read except for a dim 1800s patent date and a Cincinnati, Ohio address. Used in a scooping swathe, ample carrying handle guides the metal teeth.

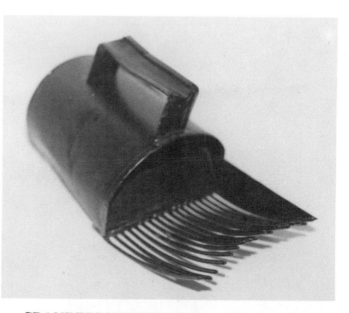

CRANBERRY SCOOP. Early; tinner lapped edges; steel teeth.

GRAPE PICKER'S HAMPER (BASKET). Iron-bound staved wood worn strapped to the worker's back; 28"H, 15" dia. at open top; 20"W.

WINE BARREL STOPPER. Handcarved wood from northwest New York State's old wineries; 3¼"H, 2" top dia.

RARE WOOL COMBS. Both were fashioned by blacksmith in the early 1700s, to draw fibers through long, sharp, round teeth into parallel slivers in making worsted yarns; and if they substituted upon occasion as flax hatchels, that was the path of the primitives; however originally intended for a special purpose, applied wherever a need arose for which they might be suitable.

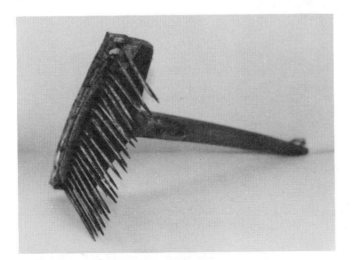

Handle and header cut from one piece of pine; spikes set in a separate narrow strip's burn augured holes were bent over about ¼" on the back; animal bone inserted between this strip and the header helped slow down warping and splintering under heavy usage; hanging eye.

Almost in miniature, hand-gripped by carefully cut polished walnut; early COMBS, CARDERS and HACKELS are not plentiful today; they were made in various sizes and types to handle differences in raw material.

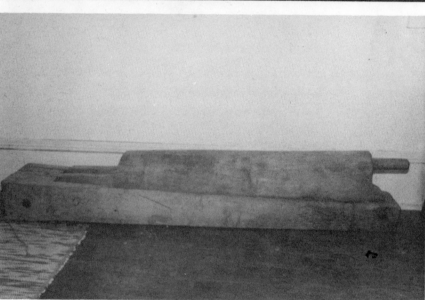

FLAX SWINGLE. (Not many of these around.) ca: 1850. To beat and clean flax, separating coarse and woody parts from softer fibers later to be woven into linen; 64½″L hardwood with 48″ top.

WOOL CARDERS. Replaced Teasels (thistles); toward the end of the 1700s machines could cut, set, and bend over short wires in long leather strips, cut to various lengths; these were fastened to wood paddles; commonly used in pairs with wool placed on one carder and the other drawn across it several times, making a fluffy mass preparatory for spinning into cloth or yarn.

FLAX KNIFE. ca: 1700s. Hand-carved; iron tab was repaired when its thin wood split with hard use; after flax brakes removed the useless sections (often kept to fill straw ticks for trundle beds), the flax was again beaten (scutched) with a wooden knife of this general form (hand swingling) to remove still more undesirable woody parts for linen; 16″L x 6″W.

FRUIT PRESS. ca: mid-1800s. Although any juicy fruit could be put into the box, customarily it was for grapes, handle pressure pushing down the heavy wood block to squeeze juice through the short tube into a pail beneath; cherry wood; from the Great Lakes region.

HONEY PRESS. ca: 1700s. Honey combs were placed in the lower section; weight of the top slowly settling down pressed honey from its wax, causing it to drip through the base holes into a container placed beneath; squared stick at lower end hand-controlled the lowering while the long pin hand-hold at the top positioned it; Michigan hickory; two natural branch front splayed legs.

Sometimes a hollow beegum log was used to lure bees, sticks wedged inside to hold the combs and holes cut for easy access in and out. On the frontiers, one way of getting honey was from Course (wild) bees. Particularly in August when the "cricks" ran low, noting the presence of winged workers, settlers spread a bait of vinegar and old honey saved for that purpose. Keeping a close watch, they could trace the bees back to their honey cache, probably in a hollow tree. Swathed in tight headcaps and shawls, they battled the bees for their sweet product. If they could manage a fire close enough, smoke temporarily deactivated the inmates long enough for their wax combs to be removed. Later, beesmokers (small hand operated bellows of tin and/or leather) became available, but homesteaders had to get honey the hard way.

BEEHIVE BOX. ca: 1800s to early 1900s. Pine; large dovetailed corners; layered inside lift-out sections for holding wax honeycombs; removable lid. When it became autumn-chilly on a Vermont farm, this box was taken into the house for the winter, taped up so the bees couldn't get out. There they remained dormant; it was so cold they'd have frozen if left outside. In the spring when the weather warmed, the box was taken outside and placed with its entries facing east. The approved time to move a hive was between sunrise and sunset.

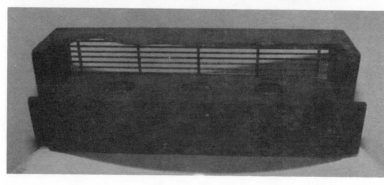

QUEEN BEE BOX. To carry her without too much disturbance to another hive, or starting a new colony, etc. (The inevitable mouse was "fixin' t' move" in.)

SORGHUM STALKS in a STAKE WAGON BED awaiting being cooked into syrup; (stalks were also processed for combining with other materials into feeds, fertilizers, etc.).

SORGHUM STALK GRINDER and HORSE (PONY). Inside gears were turned to cut, crush or pulverize the cane by small horses, tough ponies or mules slowly walking around treadmill style, harnessed to one end of a cut-to-fit log; often two animals were used, one at each end of the log. Museum displays from Indiana and Kentucky.

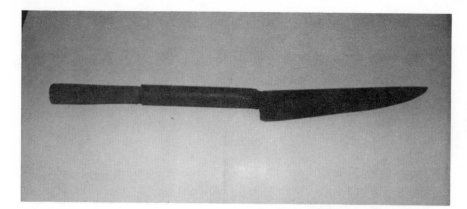

FIELD KNIFE. Iron handle and sharp blade 16½"L, wood extension 5"L.

Narrow STALK (FODDER) LEAF STRIPPER and wider CANE STALK LEAF STRIPPER. Both are made of pine showing hand-cut irregular cutting notches. They were held at smooth end and brought sharply down, knocking off dried leaves which, in the case of the FODDER STRIPPER (sometimes called a "Cornstripper") if allowed to remain when the cut up stalk was fed to livestock, could catch in their throats, choking them; 28"L and valued $22.50. The CANE or Sweet Sorghum (Sorgos) STRIPPER, sans drying leaves, was better prepared for processing; fewer of these wider ones are left; 24"L.

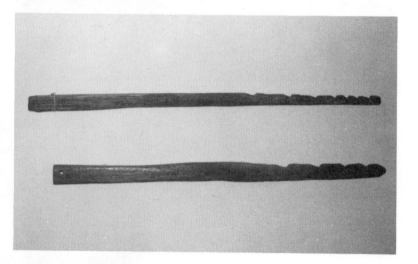

COVERED WAGON TRUNK/-BOX. Hand-cut pine, iron hinges, six-board with inside divider; lid later reinforced; carried on a covered wagon over the eastern mountains into middle Tennessee during the early 1800s; 38"L x 10"W x 14"D.

BRAKING (DRAG) SHOE. Made of iron to fit over a wagon (buckboard, stagecoach, etc.) wheel to retard progress down a steep grade or to slow down the vehicle; an Idaho rancher told me his Pa made these of wood on "their place."

GRAB for a SNATCH TEAM. ca: 1800s. As quaintly expressed, that's just what it did; temporary harnessing for one team to assist another stuck in deep mudholes, dropoffs in stream bed fordings, etc.; top ring was fastened to floundered wagon's tongue, the twisted ends hooked to traces of pulling horses or mules. This example belonged to a dedicated Steuben (and other artglass) collector who could not resist buying this one delectable primitive - and hung it on a prominent wall of his home.

GREASE BUCKET. ca: very early. Hollowed from a log; lid can be raised but is held from slipping off the rope bail by knots on the underside of the cover; kindlin' splinters or trail side small branches were always handy for slathering thick greases onto squeaking hubs and axles (tar often mixed with grease to avoid hot weather melting as the Artillery Units did it). Some bark remains petrified on the wood.

GREASE BUCKET. Bulbous staved oak that swayed along under a wagon's side or tailgate; iron bands; wire bail replaced; missing lid fit down on the inside groove.

All smithy-made from iron; old ones. DRAGHOOK (left) and CHAIN (right) worked wherever pulling was needed.

WAGONHAMMER (center). So far, these have not been hard to find, especially at rural sales; could hammer with its back or tighten wheels as a wrench; this one different with two rings rather than one, worn from being hurriedly thrust into several positions jostling along holding the singletree to the wagon; takes a long time to deepen iron ridges the blacksmith may have been asked to lightly define.

WAGON KEG. Curve-staved wood sides and iron hinged lid; wood bottom; iron bands and side handles; hole for spigot could be plugged and water dipped from the top; carried to workers. In the early days with little knowledge of sanitation, cider was substituted where water sources were unreliable or as a special treat. In the early colonies, bequeathing barrels of cider was as common as leaving household supplies and furniture.

WAGON JACKS. Patent dated Feb. 14, 1888; Wood and iron, marked: "Dandy Jack"; 30"H.

Dark stained wood; iron fixtures; 26" to top of lowered handle.

WAGON TOOL BOX. Original red paint fairly good on pine, black iron hinges and a common hook fastener; part of the farm wagon which won a Gold Medal, it is black-printed on one side: "Awarded Gold Medal Louisiana Purchase Exposition 1904 U.S.A". 6"H lid, 11"W x 11"D; slants to base 9½" x 9½".

COMB. Brass with wood handle; this one used to groom horses' tails.

ANIMAL BELL. Iron with hand-whittled wood clapper; hung on oxen early in the 1800s by settlers coming over the mountains into eastern Tennessee; wrapped seams, made by a tinner.

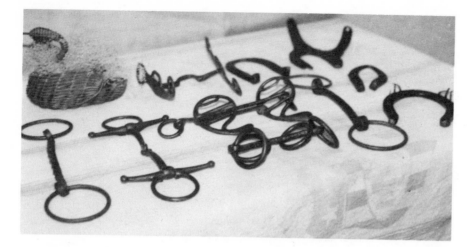

SHOES. Iron for workhorse and carriage horses, one with original nails, that at the upper corner with a forged bar to correct the gait of a pony with an orthopedic problem; farriers fit and corrected shoes individually to horses, ponies, mules and oxen for they could no more wear one standard size then do we.

BITS. All iron including twisted mule, jointed doublecheck for breaking colts, for unmanageable animals and long port bit.

UNCOMMON MULE COLLAR. Made of iron, its edges rolled to make the weight and style not uncomfortable without straw or cloth packing; hinged to install on the animal at the top and where the bottom meets and rests against the chest.

HORSECOLLAR. Still no splits expose the firm straw packing nor mar the wide leather apron, just worn from years of contact with a horse's sweating neck; even the iron locking device is usably intact.

Brass topped dogwood HAMES are in proper position to carry the greater pull of the reins.

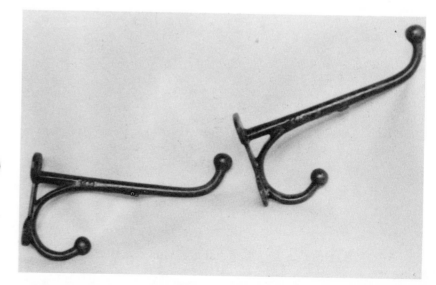

HARNESS HOOKS. All three cast iron; ball and mushroom ends kept articles from slipping off; collar hung on the heavier top hook with lighter harness below. These are severely depleted by collectors from their first original abundance; their practicality has come a long way from the barns and carriage houses.

HARNESS HORSE (STITCHER). Hand-cut from hardwood; for harness making and mending at leather shops and farms; legs' tops are slashed and firmly pinned (in the old way) through the seat for extra rigidity; a foot on the pedal activated the strap to clamp objects tightly; complete.

UNUSUAL smaller size HARNESS HORSE. Hickory legs and solid pine seat and pincers; easy for worker to operate seated on the rear of the 2″ thick board; 35″H x 24″L; skillfully made; complete.

HARNESS YOKE. A wooden bar attached by a leather, brass-studded ring to the end of a carriage tongue (or shaft) suspending it from the collars of a team. Handsomely finished hickory with iron fittings and acorn ends; not a commonly seen collectible.

HORSE ANCHOR (HITCHING WEIGHT). Cast iron; held the animal trained to respect it enough not to run away; usually fastened by a long leather strap to the bridle, it was carried in a vehicle and tossed out upon the ground when the driver had to leave for a short while; 6″ dia., 3″ H; all shapes and sizes but same idea; every horse had one - or should've.

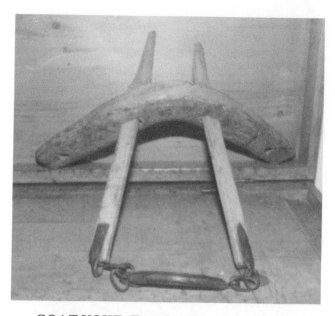

HITCHING WEIGHT (TETHER). ca: 1800s. Primitively fashioned by a smithy; weighs at least 30 lbs.; this was probably carried in a wagon to be thrown out on the ground, a leather strap through the ring attached to the wagon and the other end fastened to horse's bridle. While an animal could have walked away pulling it, it was enough of an impediment for the horse (or mule) to stand still. (In addition the horse's bridle strap might have been attached to a post.)

GOAT YOKE. Found in Massachusetts, made by a smithy; from hickory with iron fixtures; very old; 21″W.

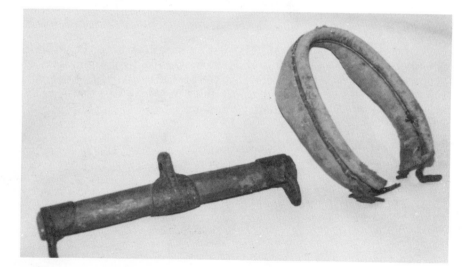

GOAT COLLAR and SINGLE-TREE. ca: latter 1800s. Harness that pulled a child's goat wagon; collar buckled at base.

CALF'S YOKE with POKE. Homemade with the yoke, a bent-wood branch with dried bark still on it; trained the little one to respect enclosure boundaries as the Poke hit fences and gates.

CALF MUZZLE. Cut by a farmer over 100 years ago; open tube in mouth allowed breathing but kept animal from it's mother's milk when it was old enough to graze; 12"W.

CALF MUZZLE. Wireware restrainer; top loop slipped over head, easily removed for feeding.

WORKHORSE SHOE. Farrier (smithy who also shod animals) fitted to the foot; original nails.

CALVES' SALTBOX. Rough tongues steadily licking at a saltblock placed inside, along with exposure to the elements, wore through the bottom of the box at least a century ago; brass studs protected the topsides of this farm-made softwood holder about 8" square; one of the pieces you'd like to hear talk.

FARM FORK. Made for a special purpose, a marriage of a (pitchfork) handle and wooden prongs said to have been part of a cranberry rake about a century ago; 30"L.

DEHORNING SHEARS. Used some years ago, this tool dehorned both range and domestic cattle so they would not butt another animal hurtfully when running freely or injure themselves when kept in close confinement; fresh stubs were painted with tar to slow any bleeding and prevent infections; here such encrustation built up by extended use has been cleaned off; wood and iron, marked: "Franklin Barum Co., Denver Col."; 62"L.

"WC" BRANDING IRON. Made by a smithy; with long handle and hanging ring; 28"L.

ELEPHANT HEAD BRANDING IRON. Wrought iron; note tusks; 36"L ring end handle; heat use evident; origin northern Florida ranching area beyond Jacksonville (known as Cowford), settled in 1816.

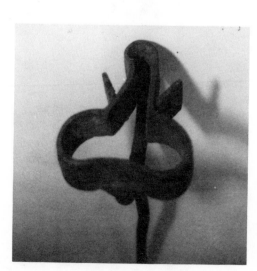

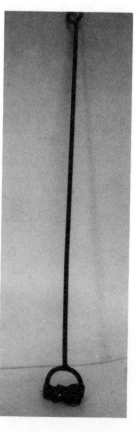

"RC" BRANDING IRON. Very old; handle gone; these were often wrought by ranch blacksmith; 6"W.

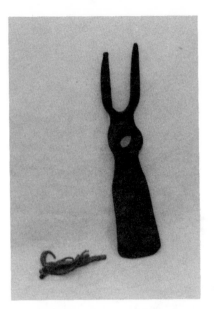

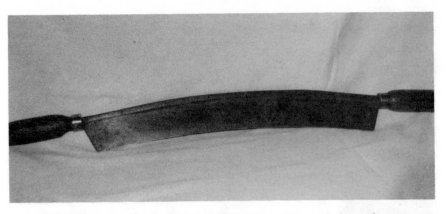

TANNER'S UNHAIRING KNIFE. ca: 1800s. Delicately concave, curved one-edge sharp blade with wood handles and brass collars; used to prepare rough hides for the currier's work.

GINSENG HOE and DRIED GINSENG ROOTS. From a general idea, but to the smithy's own or his customer's wishes, this particular hoe is long and narrow. Guided by a long wood handle held through the wide round collar, prongs loosened woodland soils and the hoe dug out roots of this perennial herb; dried and sold to the local apothecary, these aromatic medicinal additives were a source of ready cash to the farmer - or to the townsman wanting extra income.

BRICK MOLD. ca: 1800s. Triple, wood with iron bands; 5¾"W x 31"L overall; 3" D.

BRICK MOLD. ca: 1800s. Single, wood slanted one side; mortised ends into rounded corners, sides; 6¾"L x 3¾"W.

THREE VIEWS OF A RARE BRICK. ca: 1800s. Found at a Flagler Beach, Florida, shop. Clay hand fashioned of a whiter, more granite-like substance than the red clays; an Indian's head is an embossed carving on one side; that on the opposite side was never completed; one thick edge has deep carvings resembling feathers but uncertain what the lines do represent; about half an inch longer than the ususal 7½″ to 7¾″, about half an inch wider than customary 3¾″ and much thicker than ordinarily seen.

BRICKS. ca: 1800s. Clay, hand-fashioned. From a tumbling wall at a former Alabama mountain crossroads; 7½"L x 4"W x 2½"D.

BRICK. ca: 1800s. Clay hand-fashioned. Impressed: DON'T SPIT ON THE SIDEWALK; when later dawning awareness of public health hazards became fairly countrywide, a western Plains banker, in this instance, laid such a sidewalk to his doors. Clear into the 1900s, avid souvenir hunters began using crowbars at night to pry up the bricks, keeping a few for themselves, selling the others. So there, as elsewhere, a town ordinance soon decreed such acts punishable thefts; 7¾"L x 3¾"W x 2½"D. Brick Collector's Clubs are today increasingly popular.

SMALL TOOL BOX. Hand-cut from walnut; made with square nails; carrying slot is shaped for two fingers, separated with a tiny down curve making it more comfortable to carry; bottom and sides are 1" thick; overall 12¼"L x 7"W and 3¼"H without handle. Rare size.

TOOL CARRIER. Made from wood on the homeplace, saw marks; square nails; 1"D x 14"W x 8"H x 26½"L.

TOOL CARRIER. Pine with iron handle.

Two SHAVING HORSES. ca: 1800s. Each hand-fashioned from hickory. The worker used a footclamp to anchor an object, then applied a pulling action with a drawknife. The upper has slots where a wood pin held the adjustable clamp.

The lower is much older, seen stored on the Niagara Frontier in an early farm-homesteaded outbuilding long since abandoned.

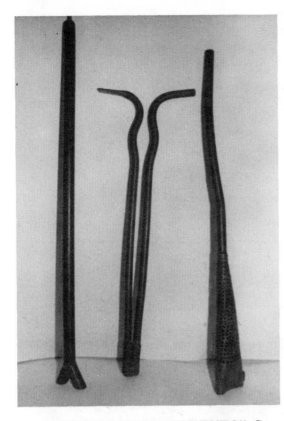

WHISKEY STILL MASHER. All wood and heavy to handle; mashed and stirred cooking brew ingredients.

WHISKEY STILL "THIEVES". Copper, siphoned-off brew for tasting, testing, whatever, as part of the apparatus for distilling illegal alcoholic liquids in "Stills". 26½″ to 30″L.

HAMMER (MALLET). Wood handle with copper double face 3″ dia. each side; weighs 5 lbs.; 15″L handle.

WHEELWRIGHT'S REAMER. ca: 1850. Sharpened on base inside of blade; using both hands to exert pressure on the handle "reamed" out tapered holes, such as in wagon wheel hubs; sizes varying up to three ft. in length. 21″W handle, 26½″ overall length.

At the Blacksmith's Shop SPECIAL PURPOSE ANVIL. Long horn in iron; set for use on a solid base, sometimes a log cut to individual working height and set upright with anvil on top.

MANTRAP. ca: 1700s to early 1800s. Smithy-made of iron; such traps were used in Europe from the 1400s for privileged landowners to catch poachers. These huge spring devices were used by a few American colonials with vast estates in New England and down along the east coast. The only way a trespasser could escape from these jaws was if a fellow poacher set him free (being caught was painful enough without the inevitable severe penalty).

PRIMITIVE CANADA GOOSE. ca: early 1800s, Maine origin. Roughly cut from a pine slab; in the beginning little attention was paid to detailing carvings other than general shaping; by the 1840s-50s carvers started adding colored feathers, etc. and personalizing the wood lures.

DECOYS. Imitating southwestern Indians of a thousand years ago, American settlers in the latter 1600s began making lures from skins stuffed with hay to entice wild birds from the skies within gunshot range, the birds a vital additional food source. These materials proved too fragile for continuing seasonal use, so whittlers and gunners along lakes and seacosts began carving the baits from white cedar, switching to white pine when the cedar became depleted. Occasionally decoys were made from canvas and papier mache. "Floaters" were anchored in open water; "Shore Birds" (Stick ups) atop wood stakes were placed in marshes and at shoreline feeding grounds, a large number of "sets" more likely to bring in a flock than just a few. (The word "Decoy" is a contraction of the Dutch EndeKooy, a cage or trap into which wild ducks were driven by men in boats, and was not commonly applied until late in the 1800s.)

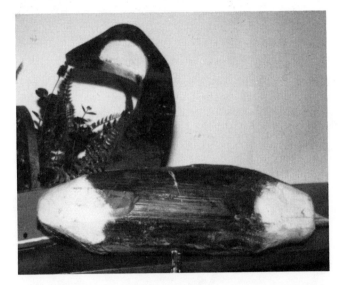

CANADA GOOSE DECOY (MARSH). Origin Prince Edward Island, Canada. Heavy solid wood block with 1¾″ thick flat head and neck; hand-cut; all original; eyes are indicated with a tiny slash in the wood; long pole for setting it out in a marsh or near shores to entice wild flyers; head and neck 12″L; 21″H without pole.

CANADA GOOSE. Origin western New York State or Ontario region; balsa; deepset metal eyes; about 21″L, tiny nick one side of bill.

CANADA GOOSE. Very old; eyes defined by cutting the wood; 28″L x 9½″W back.

SLEEPER (CONFIDENCE) DUCK (Background). Decoys did not have to be carved to represent the kind of birds being lured; sleeping (or those seen as feeding) instilled a feeling of security (or confidence) in the wild ones flying overhead seeking rest and/or feeding.

LINES OF HEAD on GOOSE.

CANADA GOOSE DECOY. From Prince Edward Island, Canada; very heavy; 31¼" from beak to tip of tail; only touch-up to original paint has been a strip of white just back of the beak; excellent feathers work; metal eyes; 12"D; placed on the four long spikes for display since bottom is rounded; solid wood.

BUFFLEHEAD DUCK (BUFFALOHEAD). So called because head had thick fluffy feathers. This example is from Currituck Sound, North Carolina; metal eyes; 9¾"L x 5½"H x 4¾" across the back; solid wood.

MAINE GOOSE. Realistically made of cardboard-type paper; label of maker inside with full assembling directions; three parts fasten at top back and base of neck that bends head down and forward; held upright by a long iron rod attached inside; for marshy ground stick-up; a number shipped flat in boxes.

CANADA GEESE, the SLEEPER and the WATCHER (included in sets is sometimes THE FEEDER.) Well-made hollow papier mache; glass eyes; heads removed, bodies nest for shipping.

MALLARD HEN. ca: 1800s. All original; feathers pattern is noteworthy, as well as the flowing, graceful lines. Age crack on solid wood.

CONFIDENCE DUCK. ca: late 1800s. BROADBILL with good clean lines, faded to a greenish hue; interesting iron strap repair adds to the value. (Sleepers in position whose bills do not touch the back are in greater demand, scarcer and more expensive.).

DUCK DECOYS. WOODDUCK testing ear of corn; one glass eye is set higher than other making a cross-eyed look. Unusual.

MALLARD HEN. ca: 1800s. Brown with realistically painted features; glass eyes.

MALLARD MALE. ca: 1890. Solid wood; shoebutton eyes.

PRIMITIVELY CARVED DUCK. From wood slab with flat head and shoebutton eyes.

CANVAS-BACK DUCK. Handsomely painted feathers; metal eyes.

FOR COMPARISON: NEW CANADA GOOSE. Marked: "Missouri Ltd." in edition of only 25 made in this design. Brightly colored; ridged feathers; solid wood.

NEW DUCK DECOYS. PINTAIL HEN. Brown head on brown and black body.

PINTAIL DRAKE. Red, white breast; vivid colors.

UMBILICAL CORD BAG (Front). In which a Sioux Medicine Man kept the dried length, traditionally, a highly respected practice among the tribes. The 8"L handsomely beaded back GILA MONSTER has a narrow aged leather strip (cut from animal skin) totecord in its mouth for easier carrying at Ceremonials. The realistic fat tail represents the body reservoir where the Gila monster stored food during hard times.

BASKET (Background). ca: 1920, Seminole. Subdued colors in natural dried grasses with pale tinted-reddish designs; 3½"H x 5½" at widest part.

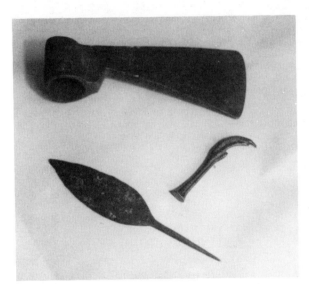

TRADE AXE. ca: 1700s. Once highly desirable trade items (particularly with the early French Explorers); folded iron to provide handle space and wide collar; impressed "RA O IV.".

PIPE TAMPER. Finely fashioned RARE TURKEY FOOT in bronze.

PIPE CLEANER. Early hand-fashioned FEATHER; reallistically marked.

POTTERY. ca: 1870s. Grayish colored VESSELS found in the Mississippi area resembling our early Mississippian culture; crushed shells were mixed with native clays, then fire tempered. Larger BOWL has side ear lifts and an impressed 1½" deep design around the rim; 6"H x 8½" at widest part.

Shallow BOWL has a pie-like edge, crimped rim design; 2"H x 6½" at widest part.

# TENDING THE HOME

FIREPLACES in colonial homes had the fullest possible assortment of kitchen tools, or the barest, but all did their best to have the basic cranes and trammels for fireplace cooking. This 1700s museum grouping has a twisted handle FORK for handling the logs, a rare long-handled SKILLET sought by collectors of such early Americana, TOASTERS, KETTLES, et al., each blacksmith-fashioned. A heavy iron door opens to reveal an oven built into the stone wall side (a smaller version of huge bakers' ovens). The adjustable SAWTOOTH TRAMMEL has a rare double hook, and there are examples of the COLONIAL HEART design on handles.

ANDIRONS (FIREDOGS). ca: 1700s. Museum display; similiar evaluations $150.00 a pair to over $200.00 a pair. Smithy-fashioned iron with popular heart. Long handled fireplace cookery SKILLET in corner is a scarce and expensive item today.

ANDIRONS. ca: 1870-1880. Cast iron; Western Kentucky origin; third generation family enjoyed.

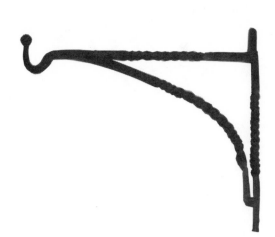

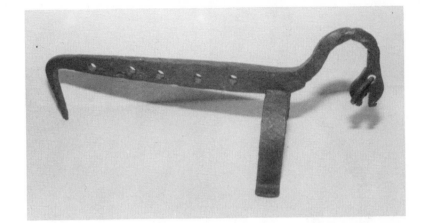

FIREPLACE SWINGING CRANE. ca: 1840-1850. Smithy-forged Southern piece that fit into iron brackets mortared into brick or stone interior side of a fireplace; held pots and kettles of bubbling foods; end mushroom kept handles from slipping off; 14¾"H. Cranes were essential in homes.

SKEWER REST. ca: early 1700s. Hand-wrought iron, twisted neck and ring mouth; overall form represents an animal; the rear and one front foot base show burn signs from having stood in hearth ashes and coals; skewers rested through the five holes or were laid with one end against the back. Skewers were iron pins to hold a piece of meat firm, fasten cuts to spits or even act as testers. (Rare).

FIREPLACE CRANE. ca: mid-1800s. Points anchored into side of fireplace; hook was a hanger for holding cooking containers.

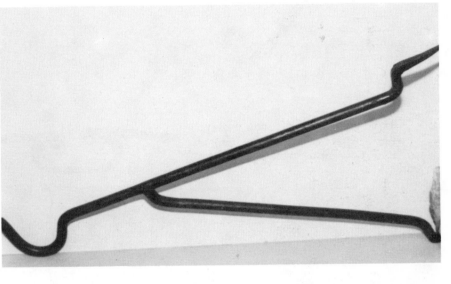

UTENSIL and/or LIGHT GAME BOARD. ca: 1700s. Thin wrought iron hooks were placed in burn-augured holes and bent over to hold firm on the reverse side of this proudly carved walnut board. In a Pennsylvania home it hung within easy reach on a wall near the fireplace; hooks were too slim for heavy cuts of meat; wood was stripped in this generation but traces of original milkbase (casein) white paint remain; 27"L x 9"W.

DOUBLE POTHOOKS. Smithy-forged; this size was more typically found hanging in Inn and estate kitchen fireplaces; very old.

HANDFORGING. Iron puzzler - owner felt part of crane-type hanger to hold pots and kettles over the coals.

GRAPPLING HOOK. Smithy-made; four sharp pointed prongs; at home the hook could've been used to bring up food tins that had slipped off ropes as they cooled down in the well (or lids that fell off); diversified uses in waters; (recently painted black).

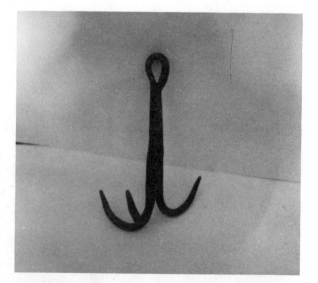

TRAMMEL HOOK. Made of iron forged by an early blacksmith, this hook is about 6½"H; could hold small pots and kettles in the fireplace and on occasion, grapple; points are fairly blunt.

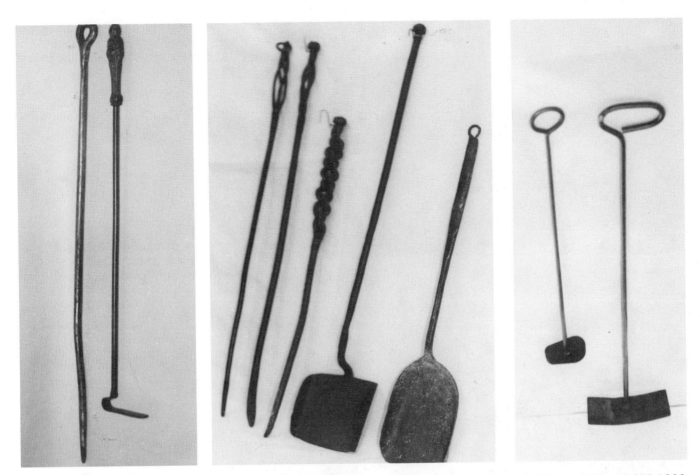

FIREPLACE ASH SHOVELS, POKERS, FLUE RAKES (latter cleaned out soot deposits). ca: 1870-1900. Cast and forged iron; plain and ornamental handgrips, one fancy top brass shaped like a long pull.

FIREPLACE POKERS. Three cast-iron brass-top iron tools.

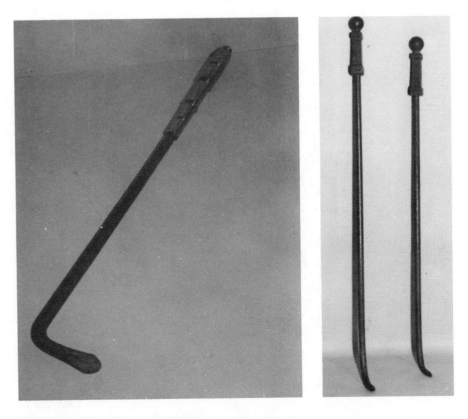

HEARTH GRILLE. Revolves; three spider legs 2″H; rattail eye-ring at end of long shaped handle; overall 18¼″L.

Two blacksmith-wrought irons for fireplace cooking, each showing skills of that particular craftsman from the 1700s.

HEARTH TOASTER. Two wide stubby feet; curled handle rest; 16¼″L x 6½″H; museum display.

TRIVET. ca: 1800s. Hand-forged; this was set in the ashes keeping cooking vessels' contents warm; this example is in a museum.

TRIVETS. Smithy-made iron 3½″H x 7″W about 6½″ dia.

This type is also called a FOOTMAN; designed brass plate, turned wood handle, cabriole iron legs; 12¼″H.

SPLINTERS BOX. ca: 1700s, early 1800s. Pine from the Virginia mountains; hung beside a cabin fireplace; slanted sides made easier "reaching in" to get pine kindlin' splinters; long extinct worms left wavery trails (now considered decorative and a big plus); box followed general style of less ample candle and long clay pipe wall holders; hand cut. (Rare).

BOOTSCRAPER. ca: 1700s. Pennsylvania hand-forged; originally mounted on the stoop of a home for scraping the soles of boots and shoes; when a hard freeze cracked the stone, the scraper was released, even though the ends had been shaped to better hold. 15″H x 10″W.

OVEN PEEL. Early smithy-made with rattail handle curve; one piece iron; a few heat marks.

CHESTNUT ROASTER. ca: 1800s. Copper rarity; style similar to a flatter bedwarmer; copper-riveted iron fixture holds movable lid and iron handle whose wood portion is gone; note irregularly punched holes with decorative raised rings-around; hand crafted in Switzerland but has been in an American collection for a long time; 19½″H x 8″ dia. x 4″D.

Name and location printed on background, a double-woven COTTON GRAIN BAG with a fish trademark.

SPRINGHOUSE. ca: 1850, museum restoration. Built of logs cut from settler's clearing; nestles below a hill in Western Kentucky near a frigid stream that trickles in and out of shallow man-made pools, where milk buckets and other food containers could be kept cool.

MILK PAILS. ca: 1800s, early 1900s. Heavy tin with strong bails (handles), the smaller example is more often seen (reproduced); the slant-sided example is more unusual.

WATER BUCKETS. Staved wood sides, the smaller example is slightly tapered to its base; a rope extends through extra long ears; this is the older of the two. Larger but still very old, the second bucket has iron bands and handle ears; both types customarily stood on handy bucket benches.

TUB. Staved wood sides taper to a wider base diameter; iron bands; two thick staves are longer carrying holds. These were made in innumerable sizes and shapes for water, maple sap, milk and cream, etc., including the PIGGINS, small wooden pails with handles of an upright stave on one side; a type of ladle for dipping out of a tub, cream pails sometimes called Piggins. And there was the FIRKIN, a wood, butter or lard measure (56 lbs.) or even a liquid measure for beer, ale, cider or perry, the latter a type of fermented pear juice.

BUTTER CHURN . . . (DASHER). Stave construction with iron bands held with rivets that do not penetrate all the way through the wood; 34½"H.

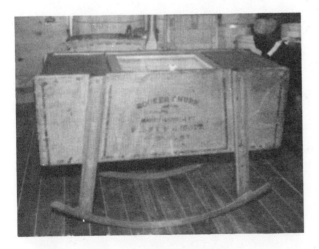

ROCKING BUTTER CHURN. Rare LOCKPORT; Patented, Manufactured By Frank Elliott; Lockport, New York; pine with pecan stain, iron rockers; side handles; blown glass, wood-framed lift-lid has a china knob; inside slots for two wood-burning paddles which could be taken out for easy cleaning; long handle, middle of rear top was for rocking operation; 22½"H without handle 32"W x 13"D.

BUTTER CHURN. Davis Swing Churn, No. 1 Patented, manufactured by Vermont Farm Machine Company, Bellows Falls, Vermont; maple barrel with glass in knob-lift top; handle each side; iron fixtures; oak stand; churn 30"W x 10"D x 12¾" tall x 40½"H overall; original mustard yellow paint with black trim.

KEELER. ca: 1800s. Amish-made; keelers were shallow hooped tubs which hastened the milk-cooling process; also were used to wash butter with cold water after it was taken from a churn; a very old type of container originating in Europe; here taller-than-usual side handles are carved as extensions of the thick heavy wood staves; brad-fastened wide-iron bands; 12″ dia.

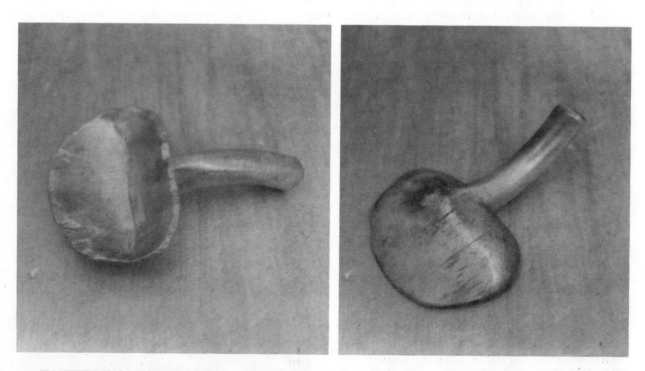

BUTTERWORKER (SCOOP). ca: 1700s. New England maple; one piece hand carved, dished inside 1½″ down from handle, conforming to highest ridge on back; comfortable wide-arched handle easily held; 5¼″ widest part of scoop; has evidence of being thumped against containers to shake off bits of butter; weight ⅞ oz., 8″L overall.

BUTTER CARRIERS. ca: 1800s. Pennsylvania origin. Pine; each one piece lid has whittled-out handholds and is tightly held by pins in side slots; the smaller example is earlier, with "fancy-top" ears, 7½" top dia., bulbous staves 9¼"H, has shaved hickory locked-lap hoops (ash and oak were also used) that slip under each other and won't ease apart. At some time a 6½"L x ¾"W metal strip was nailed on the rim where hitting with butter scoops must have broken off staves' tops.

The larger 11" top dia., 10¾" slanted staves has a 1"W heavy iron band and a 1½"W thin iron band near the top, probably added later, each band held by the ends smithy-hammered together, small nails were added later that don't penetrate through the wood to spoil the butter.

Butter that wasn't needed for home use was packed for bartering or market. Such tubs as these carried the larger quantities, packed with a flat-head masher (tamp) and leveled off with wood knives.

BUTTER BOWL and WORKER (PADDLE). Paddle dated 1889. ca: 1800s. Both hand-tool and lathe-fashioned; maple and pine; Kentucky origin; bowl flat at center of base with rolled sides; paddle with hanging eye; museum display.

BUTTER MOLD. ca: 1800s. Maple; four removable sections of two prints each stamped for decorating and the owner's identification with a rope border and the letter "M".

CHEESE MIXING BOWL and CURDS KNIFE. Hand-cut wood oval bowl with slight grooves where cutter might have regularly rested; in this the drained cheese base was salted and mixed for pressing.

The KNIFE is four parallel flexible blades held in a wood handle; for cutting drained chunks called "curds".

CHEESE CURD BREAKER. ca: 1850-1860. Hand-cut wood with each pin intact; red stain still very good; set on boards, hand-turning the crank broke up bigger chunks of coagulated milk into smaller curds; these and liquids dropped into a container set below; carved eye for wall storage; Midwest origin.

CHEESE KEEPER. ca: 1700s-early 1800s. Tin finial on wire cover that protected the cheese from insects; round 6″ dia. edge-grooved pine base still has the "greasy" feel from the cheese it once held.

CHEESE DRAINER with its own attached CHEESE LADDER. ca: 1700s. Shaker-made from pine, wood-pegged; Windsor round sticks slope in at base; rather than the more usual separate ladder, this drainer is originally attached to its own; with cheesecloth placed in the basket, the wet mixture was poured in, then set over a large crock to catch whey dripping from the coagulated chunks of milk.

CHEESE DISH (KEEPER). Lightly glazed ironstone; items with cows are very desirable, this with it's full animal finial exceptionally so; minutely detailed embossing with a twisted ring design around the ruminating cow; 12¼″ dia. x 11½″H; treasured and used by a Tennessee family for several generations.

CHEESE DRAINER. ca: 1830. Thick curved wood staves held by two wide iron bands drained whey from curds; 8⅝″ top dia. x 3¼″H.

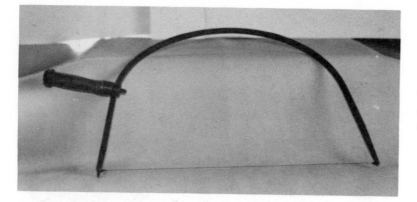

CHEESE CUTTER. Wood handle with brass collar, cutting edge is thin wire bow; could have been used at table in a home, Inn, etc.

LIDDED PANTRY BOX. ca: 1800s. Small sizes generally were used for sugar, butter, herbs, spices, medicinal roots and the like. Sometimes lingering smells will tell. 2½"H x 4" dia.

CHEESE HOOP. "C" and "H" letters appear on nail-fastened, wrapped wood; "G" cut into base inside; 11½" dia. x 6¾"H.

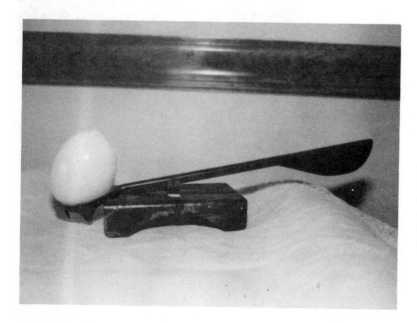

EGG WEIGHER. Traces of black finish, 6¾"L.

HEN'S EGG. Milk glass, blown, the rough base pontil (punty) mark left when glassmaker's holding and working rod is detached; the scar can also occur when pressed glass is removed from a mold with a pontil rod. Larger duck and geese eggs are available.

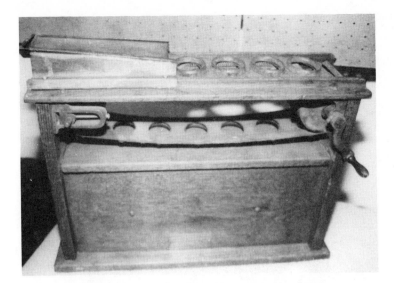

EGG SORTER. "The Electric Daylight Egg Tester manufactured by Jennings Mfg. Co., Ann Arbor, Michigan, #2124, Patented October 8, 1912"; printing still clear; 20"L x 8"W x 16½"H; hand-turned; wood box with iron fixtures and a tin slide onto the testing slots; used on farms or wherever quantities of eggs needed to be handled.

APPLE PARER. ca: 1700s. Sharp blade, free moving wheel on wire pulley; wood fork used to push pared fruit into BURL BOWL set beneath.

APPLE DRYING RACK. ca: 1800s. Pared and cut-up apples were spread out on this slatted wood dryer, the whole then set close to the hearth, sun dried, or in the loft of a home. With legs removed from their slots, the dryer could be hung on rafter hooks. One bushel of fresh apples made about seven lbs. of "Schnitz" (dried apples), enough for a family with plenty left for town bartering.

APPLE BUTTER PADDLE. ca: 1800s. Hand-cut with 2½" x 3" carved-out heart; holes allowed thickening cooking sauces to slip through for easier stirring; braced 61"L handle; 4¼" widest part; paddle 23"L cherry wood.

YARD KETTLE. Copper with iron reinforcing its rolled rim and making its bail, hooked into rather small side ears; could be used on a tripod; found on a plantation. Very large and very early.

YARD KETTLE. ca: 1800s. From Wisconsin, possibly for cooking applebutter or lard. Copper with dovetailed seams and iron under-rim-roll and bail, large ears; smithy-forged stand; few dents.

NUTMEG GRATER. Wood, wire and tin; maker marked: "THE EDGAR," patent dated Aug. 18, 1891; seen in varying forms and sizes, these are generally regarded as graters for the aromatic East Indian kernel of the mace; the nut, held by the pressure spring, can be pushed back and forth or from side to side against the sharp teeth, the grater held by the underside handle; the fibrous outside nut covering (shell) is the more pungent MACE, also a spicey flavoring; three complete nuts shown. (Tiny graters were carried in weskit pockets and purses to grate nutmegs at tables where food was bland; and interestingly, many who loudly decried using snuff - used a grater in private to make (and use) that pulverized tobacco.

DIPPER. Polished iron with socket for a wood handle but could also have been used "as is"; early New England origin; rare large size indicates it was handy for dipping lard from big yard kettles.

EATING TRAY (BOWL, DISH). ca: early 1800s. Pine; set at center table in an Alabama slaves' cabin, everyone dipped in with small bowls, paddles, gourds or ladles; with spoons being non-existent to so many, they made scoops of their fingers, transferring the food directly to their mouths. The bowl held grits and other meal mixtures, vegetables, rice and sometimes meats.

DOUGHRAISER (BOWL). A very early one roughly cut from chestnut in Western Kentucky; mismatched ears, one with hanging eye; sits on a lopsided bottom; 22″L. Colonists prized the burl, the cankerous outgrowth knot on semi-hard or hard wood such as ash, walnut or maple; used for making bowls by applying a hollowing chisel and/or a lathe.

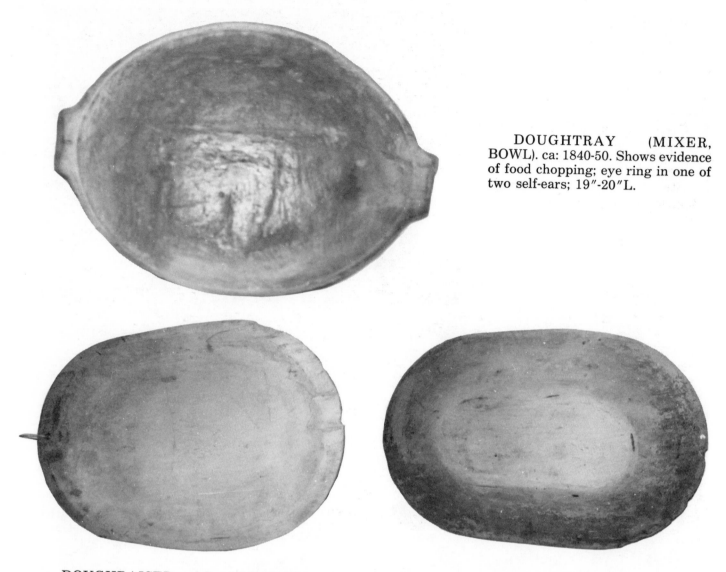

DOUGHTRAY (MIXER, BOWL). ca: 1840-50. Shows evidence of food chopping; eye ring in one of two self-ears; 19"-20"L.

DOUGHRAISER and flat UNDERSIDE desired by collectors. ca: 1850. Well-used soft-wood bowl with chipped edges where mixing utensils had been struck to shake off sticky stuff; 17"-18"L x 6½"D.

ROLLING PINS. ca: 1860. All hand-cut with age-rich patinas from one piece maple, poplar or cherry; the largest is hard maple, about 20"L, for "heavy" or bakers' dough; the three center ones are of birdseye maple, 16" to about 18"L; the rare cherry pin is 15½"L; the smallest is poplar about 12"L. Reproductions are everywhere, but the "feel" is softness and lightness from age and smoothness from wear. New wood, no matter how disguised by shellac, etc. is unmistakably fresh as compared to old.

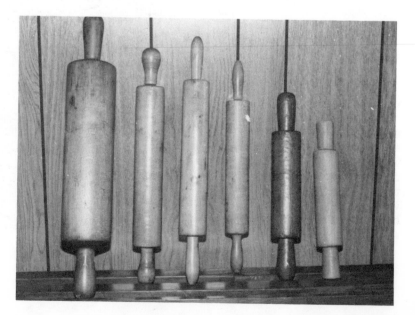

**SHAKER DOUGH ROLLER SET.** ca: 1800s. Tinned-iron pastry rolling sheet with rolled-up groove at bottom to hold wood-handled rolling pin when the set was idle; a thick wire frame continues into a loop for hanging. (Rare).

**DOUGH (PASTRY) BOARD.** Handcut pine with three-sided raised gallery; set on a table or doughbox for rolling pastry; has a "critter-gnawed" corner; 24½" square.

**DOUGH BOX ROLLING BOARD.** Originally this board was inside a lidded (probably legged) doughbox. Meal and/or flour or both were kept in divided sections and mixed and rolled on this surface; bordered wood about 26"L x 24"W.

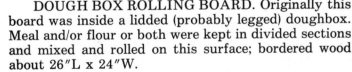

STRAINER-FUNNEL. Burnished tin uncommonly "petal dished" around tiny wire mesh at center; liquids dripped through the long base tube.

Two cherry hand-whittled FOOD PADDLES made long ago on a Mennonite farm in Ontario, Canada; 12"-15"L.

CABBAGE CUTTER (SLICER). Sharp, two-edge metal blade is angled across an 11½"W poplar board with a curved worker's seat; this was over a container; a head of cabbage was placed in a box held by side grooves and pushed back and forth. The cabbage became slivers and dropped through as our familiar "cole slaw." Small cutters made daily amounts while this large 50"L type usually was used to produce "Sauerkraut" (the cabbage juices aiding salt in forming its own brine) for home consumption and/or bartering. Kraut was first a French delicacy, then spread into Germany, and became a national delight.

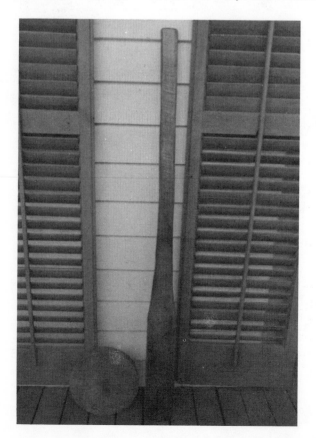

FOOD PADDLE. Hand-cut, 40"L; Food paddles were made in innumerable sizes and variations.

KRAUT WEIGHT. Thick, very heavy wood with a small metal lift ring that couldn't penetrate the wood because it would taint the food; often field stones were washed and used with cheesecloth between them and the cabbage.

FOOD KNIVES (CHOPPERS). ca: 1700s. Both Pennsylvania Dutch smithy-made, one with an extra heavy blade through a slanted handle with wood wormholes. Impressed touchmark (earmark) one side of an iron curve is a crooked triangle, the Pennsylvania Keystone framing a flower; 6¼"H overall, blade ⅜" thick.

The wider blade, almost 4¾"W, was made about 1830-40; its handle has been burn-augered through, with much of the metal bent over on top for firmness.

When buying, examine articles such as these for touchmarks indicating the stamp of the individual or group of makers.

CHOPPING KNIVES. Single and double tangs of iron or steel on shaped wood handles; a slim band of steel is added to the shiny one; there are impressed dot eyes on the fanciest with birds' heads curves; the half-moon blade with slanted handle has a Pennsylvania Keystone touchmark; sizes vary from 5" to 6½"L; 4⅝" the widest part. It would be rare indeed to find two of these smithy-made choppers exactly alike; these were among the busiest of home tools since food had to be preserved for future meals as well as prepared daily.

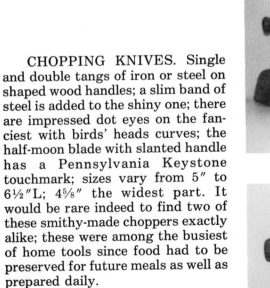

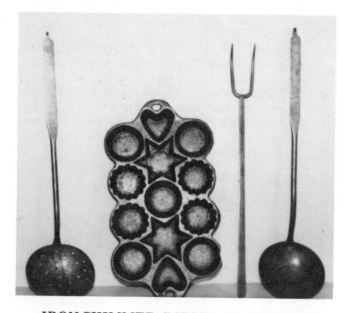

IRON SKIMMER, DIPPER, FORK. ca: 1800s. Smithy-made.

PASTRY MOLD. Cast iron, no maker's marks.

FLOUR BARREL and Sugar Cone. Hickory stave sides, iron hoops, typical gnawed entry at rim, new lid; (cone bought at Williamsburg, Virginia).

SUGAR GRINDER. Maple, dovetailed corners; tin funnel top with wood knob handle, brass drawer pull; iron inside gears; for coarse (basin) sugar; 4½" base to 3¼" top.

WOODENWARE . . . all very early pieces.

TANKARD. This is considered to be from an affluent home; checkerboard woven slanted strips on a solid base. Tankards are almost never seen without lids; wide squared bentwood handle lifts solid hinged lid which follows the spout's curve, anchored by a wood pin slipped through the eyeholed upright near the nose to forestall spilling. Used as a drinking vessel, (similar to a noggin but not used at tables) for making hot toddies, etc. This was found in the western Lake Ontario region.

FLOUR SIFTER. Tiny wire-mesh screen brass-anchored on each side of the roll; four-walled open-bottom box set by wood projections over a container, allowed flour to sift down without misting out when the iron handle was turned by its wood handgrip.

CHEESEKEEPER. See page 55.

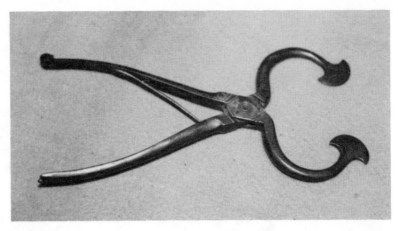

POLISHED NIPPERS. 8″L spring handle CLEAVERS kept on sugar chest to snip off bits of refined white (tea) sugar sold in indigo blue dyed paper wrapped cones, the paper fine for tinting cloth. Even today at various Inns in France, West Germany and Holland, bowls of coarsely ground basin (brown) sugar appear on tables regularly with salt and pepper.

Miscellaneous Patterns MOLDS SET in miniature. One dozen tiny tin cutters in a lidded box; could've been used for tea cookies.

MAPLE SUGAR MOLDS. ca: 1700s to early 1800s. Pine, plain hearts, one with anchor center; hand-carved in New England; hardened maple syrup chunk forms were released from the wood, retaining their designs.

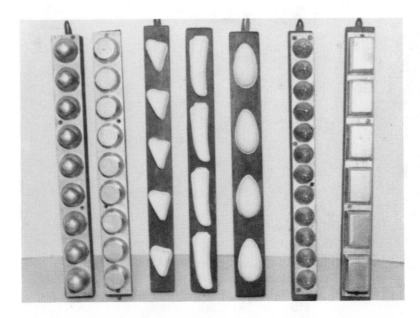

CANDY MOLDS. For chocolates and creams in colors, all mounted to display on wood; the smallest one made old-fashioned chocolate drops.

MOLD. Very heavy copper pan with handles and ring-lift lid which would indicate use with heat; could be for fancy tea cookies; 12 spaces of fish, shell, butterfly, geometrics and more; 8½″ dia. x 1¾″ D; owner uncertain of exact use.

DIVIDED ROASTER. ca: 1800s. Tin with heavy wire handles; 15″L x 12″W at center.

CUP. Hinged lid; small drinking spout with screw-on cover.

FUNNEL. Very old rolled and wrapped seams from tin; mallet marks; strap handle is bent, its inverted cone base is gone, but it still has a lot of character.

POSNET. ca: 1800s. Tri-footed deep skillet/pan with eye ring handle and smithy-crafted legs with signs of having stood many times in hot coals, raked out on the fireplace hearth for cooking; 5¼″ dia. x 4″H pan only.

TUMBLERS. Tin; wrapped seams; 5½"H x 3¾" top dia. tapering to 2¾" base dia.

LUNCH PAIL. Chain-held lid on metal container; ears might have had a carrying rope. 7" across top, about 4"H.

CHUCKWAGON PAN. Tin; four corners pulled out for better pouring of grease, gravy, etc. by the ranch cook out on cattle drives and round-ups.

Large TIN FUNNEL 7¾" dia.

Small TIN FUNNEL 5" dia.

SCRAPPLE PAN. ca: 1800s. Pennsylvania Dutch; tin; 3"H x 12" x 14".

DISHPAN. Tin; found at a former resort hotel in the Ozark Mountains, 10" dia. x 5"H.

OPEN ROASTER. ca: 1800s. Pennsylvania Dutch tinner's imperfect oval with lapped end; wire handles; 4″H x 12″ x 16″.

ALL OF PENNSYLVANIA ORIGIN. ca: 1800s.

REDWARE JAR. Tin lid lost; lead glazed inside and out in dark brown.

SLIPWARE PITCHER. Redware decorated with a semi-liquid clay paste called "Slip"; in white on uneven treasure.

SLIPWARE PLATE. About 8″ dia.; looped design slip worn almost indistinct.

REDWARE MOLD. Inside glaze; very old.

PIE PLATES. ca: 1800s. All used by Pennsylvania Dutch cooks, but such sturdy earthenware shows only one small no-harm nick on one rim.

REDWARE. Lead glazed inside; 8″ dia. x 1¾″H.

YELLOWWARE. Inside has a crude dull brown glaze; 7″ dia. x 1¾″H.

YELLOWWARE. Light brown inside glaze; desirable small size; 5¾″ dia. x 1½″H.

American pottery was made on farms all over the country, wherever there was suitable clay and wood to fire kilns. Settlers provided utilitarian wares for their families and sold the extra pottery. Made by the colonials soon after 1610, REDWARE commands high prices today, but YELLOWWARE is fast closing the gap.

YELLOWWARE. ca: 1800s. Very fine condition with good wear signs; relief moldings under clear glaze; 8½" top dia. x 5"H round on 3¼" square bottom; drapery design on overhang 1"W rim and four draped points almost touching a ¾"W blue band and two rose pink ¼"W each; little inside crazing.

PUDDING BOWL. ca: 1800s. English origin; inside light tan glaze, outside shiny brown; beading 1¼" from rolled overhang rim easy for holding; 10" top dia., 6¾" dia. base, 6½"H.

STONEWARE CROCK. Marked: "White's, Utica, N.Y."; cobalt (blue) bird on branch, attached side handles missing; 9½"H x 10" dia. x 1¾"W rim with small chip.

STONEWARE CROCK. ca: 1800s. Hand-thrown on a wheel; dull brown inside glaze; one tiny no-harm defect can be seen on one side; 8¾" dia. x 7¼"H tapering to base.

CHOP PLATE. ca: 1800s. Ironstone, KT&K's Hotel China, East Liverpool, Ohio. 6"L oval x 4"W; weighs one pound.

STONEWARE JUG. ca: 1800s. Blue swirled design; outside and inside clear glaze with cinder underglaze at shoulders and outer side of square applied handle; Pennsylvania origin.

STONEWARE JUGS. The large example Patent dated Jan. 24, 1882; mold stackmark unglazed top, center; type of BATTER JUG which might've also been used for cider or vinegar; inside dark brown glaze, outside varigated browns; natural clay base; cap or cork stopper gone.

The small jug is printed with trademark crown, name and address of Buffalo, N.Y. wholesale wine and liquor dealer; 9″H x 5½″ dia. base; made in two sections, narrow ledge where brown glazed top joins white base.

MOLD, GRANITEWARE. Thin iron with gray-speckled enamel coating; 4½″ x 6″ oval; fluted sides with ball base edging; inside bottom has well defined kernels on corn ears at each side of stalk; this design will appear impressed in the top of food from the mold when it is inverted ready to serve.

TIN CUP hung on a pump ready for anyone to use; wire handle continues under the rolled rim for strength.

CANDLESTICK; white enamel on iron, fusing into deep green; 6″ dia. x 2½″H; minor chips.

LITTLE BUCKET. White-speckled deep blue; strong side ears hold bail; this piece has many chips; 3¼″H x 4″ top dia.; 3″ at base; has been roughly handled but still a darlin' of a piece.

GRANITEWARE PITCHER. White enameled iron, no-harm chips at top and bottom handle joinings and where thumb has grasped its top; generous pouring lip; 11″H overall, 6″ base dia. tapering to 5″ overall dia. top, (dried baby's breath). Mass produced, green swirl, brown and purple are the most unusual graniteware colors found, while decorated examples and those with wood and/or wire bails are usually more expensive. Rarely is a perfect piece found since the ware was easily chipped.

DOORSTOP (DOOR PORTER). ca: 1800s. Cast iron Colonial Lady in worn but still pretty colors; hollow back; initials impressed "LBL"; 10″H x 5½″W base; door porters made from the 1790s, mainly to hold open doors to admit cooling breezes.

Two HOUSEHOLD MORTARS and PESTLES. ca: 1790-1840. Both examples are hand-carved, the first is a double cup with a solid center, so it could be inverted and used at either end. The second is made of walnut and shows hard use and decorative intent; both pulverized and pounded all sorts of foods, herbs, spices, salt, sugar lumps, etc; coffee was first "ground" by being crushed in such mortars; pestle 8″L, mortar 4″H, top dia. 5¼″ tapering to base dia. 2½″.

LAP COFFEE GRINDER. Pine; dovetailing, wood knob; iron drawer pull, handle; inside grinders operable and sliding top embossed "IMPERIAL" on one side, "EAGLE" on the other, eight brass nailheads; 5"H x 6¾" square. Base replaced.

COFFEE GRINDER. Generally a home model; wood with dovetailed corners; tin baseplate; screw cap for top filling; iron fixtures; embossed handle has wood knob; pullout drawer for ground beans.

WALL HANGING COFFEE GRINDER. Glass jar for beans; iron grinding gears inside round iron box turned by wood-knobbed iron handle; the usual tin cup catcher is gone, replaced with a table glass that fits the frame nicely; about 14"H.

CAST IRON TRIVETS above and below grinder.

COFFEE POT (SERVER). Thoughtfully designed, this rarity with a pheasant finial (peak ornament), has fluted sides tapering from bottom to top, brass hinged lid, swirled handle and a large spout.

TEAKETTLE. ca: 1800 to 1900. Copper, graceful iron handle, wood grip; it's a chubby little piece with a no-nonsense spout.

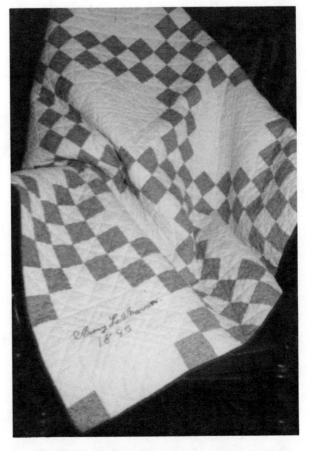

SAUCEPAN. ca: 1800s. Heavy copper; handle has hanging eye and large riveted iron band and handle.

PAPERWEIGHT. ca: 1800s. Hand-carved from one piece of walnut; polished; weighs one pound; cutout design on ledge ends; 1″ thick base 3″L x 2½″W.

BROOM HOLDER. Wireware petals on wood wall hanger; 5″H overall; old.

QUILT. dated 1890. Signed: "Mary L. Merritt". Entirely hand-stitched, red and white, clean, no deterioration; 84″ x 83½″.

SCRUBBER (SCOURING) BOXES. ca: 1800s - the lighter wood could be earlier. Principally used for cleaning knives (new one for illus.); homecut; on the frontiers, sand was the scrubbing ingredient (and pumice wherever available); both approx. 11"L x 4¾"W x 4"D.

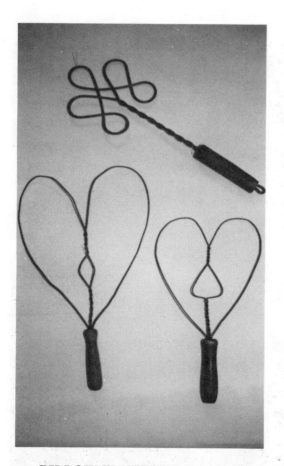

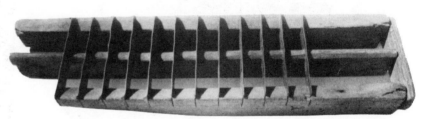

LYE SOAP CUTTER. Three 3¾" pine lengths with twelve 4½"L iron strips fit into notches at irregular 1" spacings; one hand-press down end is worn off; it made 22 bars 2¾" thick; fashioned by an early Louisiana homesteader to simplify time and energies expended in knifehacking off rough chunks of homemade lye soap laid out in a flattened slab to dry.

PILLOW FLUFFERS. Wireware; used to fluff up feather pillows commonly seen on beds having feather ticks (mattresses); wood handgrips; (reproductions being made).

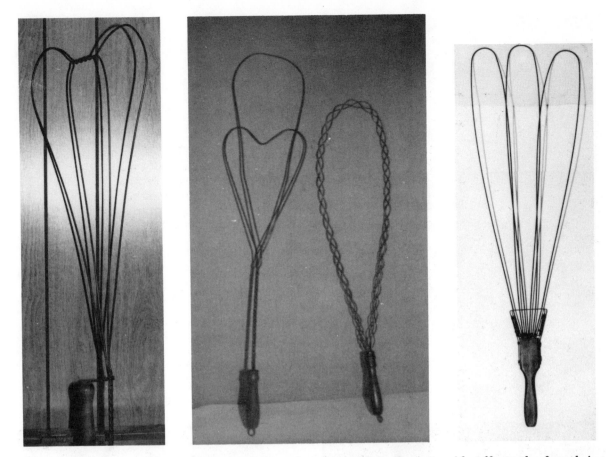

CARPET BEATERS. Wireware; three have wood handles, one side offset, the fourth is iron.

All wood SHAKER CARPET BEATER, about 30"L. These were so popular that they were finally sold outside Shaker villages.

POSE' STICK (DOLLY PEG). Ontario, Canada origin, hardwood; a step forward from washing bats (aptly named Battlin' Sticks) used for beating grease, sweat and dirt stains from rough frontier garments. Yet it still took stamina pushing clothes up and down and around, agitating them in boilers and tubs; short handle; about 35"H.

WASHING PEG. Another Dolly Peg style, all wood-fastened; two circles, each with three strong pins moving in reverse, the top loose to move up and down in thrashing dirty clothing about.

Two DOLLY PEGS. The lighter example, made of hard maple and the darker one of mixed woods have a basic pattern with factory differences apparent; about 36″H; using the handles, clothes could be stirred Hend tumbled around in a washtub or boiler.

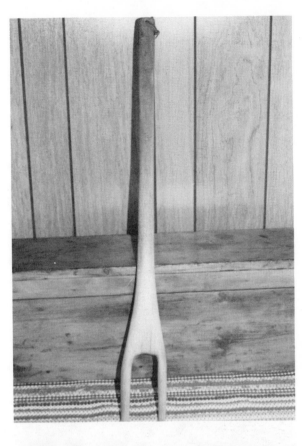

WASHSTICK. Very old; homemade from hard maple to swish clothes around and lift them out of tub or boiler; 6"L fork prongs are end-splintery-mashed and stick is base whitened from the soaps; overall about 34"L.

SCRUB (WASH) BOARD. Homemade a long time ago in North Carolina; pine with thick iron scrubbing wires at front, pushed through burned holes and tautly bent over on the back. A tin strip completes the reverse side. Another tin strip was nailed in the depression at the front top where wood cross-pieces above the wire's slightly raised wood base made a leaning ledge above and a soap ledge below.

Three SCRUB BOARDS. ca: 1800s. Hand-fashioned; the first, made of very heavy wood, was seen along Florida's Gulf Coast; about 34½"H x 14"W at top tapering to bracket feet; one piece wood with set on sides; reflects French styles.

The board on the wall is poplar with two scrubbing sections held by one-piece sides; narrow grooves for lighter or general washing.

The darker, heavier wood board is by far the earliest, its very large scrubrolls indicating they had to handle dirt encrusted rough (homespun) workclothes; there is much wear and staining where the legs rested against the edge of a tub.

WASHBOILER. ca: 1880-1890. Copper polished to its original shade; rare form with squared and curve-squarish groove trimmed on two sides; Illinois origin; iron lid-lift; after clothes were boiled, they could be swished back and forth by paddles.

SADIRONS (LAUNDRY). The small iron is for sleeves, shoulders or any hard to reach garment spots; about 5″-6″L. The everyday use iron, about 6″L, has been painted too thick to read maker's name embossed on the handle. Both are cast iron with applied handles.

SADIRONS. Laundry irons; to warm and smooth over clothes; each has blacksmith-replaced handle when the original burned off after constant use and heat.

IRONING BOARD. Wood with iron hinges; could be a stool, small table in the kitchen, and folded for storage.

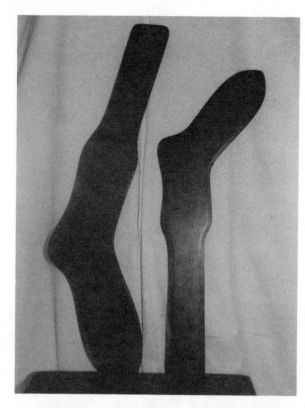

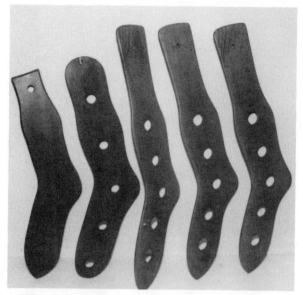

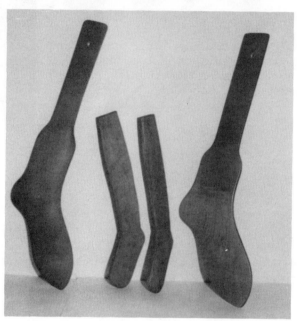

STOCKING and SOCK FORMS. Maple; some with beveled edges and impressed factory names, addresses and sizes at tops; child's set hand-whittled over 100 years ago by a Mennonnite on a farm in Ontario, Canada. Rare oversize. Those of solid wood (mostly factory used) are shapers, while those with holes most often seen in homes are dryers.

COAL SAVER. Indiana origin; unusual with double walnut hoops for unbroken iron wire mesh; well cared for despite rigorous ash-and-coals-sifting for still-burnable bits of coal in the cook or parlor stoves; and it's an old one.

KEROSENE STOVE RESER-
VOIRS. Both blue tinted glass with
screw on brass top having release
valves; attached to the end of a stove
in this position; decoratively sought
today, they are set in reverse on their
flat bottoms; these are embossed:
"Patented July 1, 1913" and
"Patented June 24, 1919" and "June
15, 1920"; iron bands and bails.

BASKETRY....'"the art of" weaving, coiling and sewing vessels from pliable wires, rushes, rope, twigs,
cornhusks, roots, strips of hides, bamboo, soft willows called osiers, along with splints from oak and ash; the
name of "BASKET WEAVERS" was given to a southwestern American culture (later our Pueblo Indians)
who covered rush baskets with clay, baking them, as early as 1500 B.C. This functional primitive folk art
advanced for centuries, baskets thrown away when they became too "dog eared". Collectibility and prices
were advancing rapidly about 15 years ago when brought to the attention of the public, but prices have now
leveled off a bit. Handmade examples are available from the latter 1800s into about the turn of the century,
factory objects not so eagerly sought. (Heights do not include handles.).

FLOWERS GATHERING
BASKET. ca: 1800s. New England
origin; tightly woven ash splint with
extra long carved handle.

MARKET BASKET. ca:
1900-1925. Rectangular with heavy
braided rim and wrapped wood
handle.

GARDEN BASKET. ca: 1800s. Virginia
origin. Splint with carved handle continuing
to bottom for strength and rigidity; 11½"
dia. x 6½"H.

EGG (UTILITY) BASKET. ca: 1800s.
Virginia origin. Oak splints woven in slightly bulbous shape with x-wrapped carved handle set in weave to base; demi-john bottom;
dark stain. Original staining or paint (even
traces) command higher prices, blue most
popular, more if combined with red and green
or bittersweet shadings, and those in dark
stains; 10½" dia. x 6"H.

GATHERING BASKET (with additional view of base). Three oak runners on woven checkerboard bottom give added strength and more level handling; strap handle; one use was for garden produce (open weaves let air in and dampness out, especially good on storage baskets).

OVAL BASKET. 14″ end to end, heavy braid rim and bottom; firm construction; found in Virginia.

RYE STRAW BASKET. ca: 1800s. The grain was raised, harvested, soaked and coiled on a Pennsylvania farm; held with age-darkened (this patina to be noted when buying) oak splints and wrapped rim; rare iron handle; these are being reproduced without this uncommon handle; 11″ dia. about 7″H.

Three BASKETS. ca: 1800s. Two very small.

BUTTOCKS BASKET. New England origin, oak splint, 8″ across; now holds woolen yarn balls.

DECORATIVE slant sides, three-strand braided tim; table basket.

TABLE BASKET. Used for "pone chunks" and biscuits; also might have held "rizing" doughs; loosely woven white oak splints.

PANTRY/TABLE BASKET. ca: 1800s. Loosely woven splint with single-wrapped hickory rim band; one side intact but broken on the other, exposing the bare wood band; bowed handle; still attractively shaped although worn; "kicked-up" demi-john bottom permitting more even distribution of such easily-broken-or-bruised contents as eggs and tomatoes; 11½" dia. x 4½"H; Virginia origin.

TABLE BASKET. Miniature; dark stained; double strand-braided rim; very old.

BASKET CARRIER. Holder in stained wood slats for six individual pint boxes of fruit; seen in Michigan.

APPLE BASKET. Oak staves curve from a turned-pine solid bottom; bentwood bail; wrapped over rim strip for holding stave tops in position; lower wire reinforcement; 15" top dia. x 9"H.

FIELD BASKET. Hand gathering cotton in Alabama fields, pickers first dropped the bolls into sacks (coarse homespun and later burlap) dragged along; when full, the contents were dumped into these large baskets sitting at the ends of long rows or in wagons; wide woven splint with heavy wrapped rim; being reproduced.

FISHING BASKET. Usually associated with trout fishing; tightly woven willow with double woven base edge; leather bound with strapping and wide shoulder sling; lift-top catch and open square for dropping in catch.

Miniature (LUNCH) PICNIC BASKET. ca: 1800s. Missouri origin; tightly woven with willow/ash wrapped handle; two lift sides on crosspieces; 8″ oval top x 6″W at center; 6¾″ oval bottom.

WIRE FIELD BASKET. Wood handgrips, origin western New York state; for harvesting onions, and other vegetables; four sides, base and rim reinforced with heavier wire; 18½″ dia. x 12″H.

WIRE STORE BASKETS. Reinforced as the Field Basket but with iron bail and wood grip; held eggs and a variety of edibles; 18½″ dia. x 12″H.

"GO CART" BASKET. Wicker, one of the first; combination chair and stroller Patented May 20, 1902; handle pulls back and down to put in (car or) carriage; about 31½″H.

SCHOOLGIRL ART BOX. ca: 1800s. Dovetailed corners, plain inside; outside: chambered top, brass-hinged, held with cotter pins. 3⅝″H.

BOX. ca: 1700s. Wood, original brass key in the hand-whittled lock with brass keeper; single top drawer has two brass pulls; painted mustard yellow designs on black; about 18″L x 10″H x 9½″W.

BALLOT BOX. ca: 1880-90. Used in a Northeast Florida County's elections; contrasting woods; lid slot for votes; 15″H x 16″W x 14″D.

SHIPPING BOX. Thought to have come into Boston Harbor in the 1800s; black printing on natural pine; dovetailed corners, later reinforced with nails; off center iron latch lock with key cutout at center; hinged lift-lid and rope handles on two sides.

"TILL" BOX. ca: 1800s. Solid mahogany, brass fittings; used for daily receipts at a tobacconist's shop; four dovetailed drawer corners with inside compartments; spring bars to hold paper money; 18" x 9".

DESK/COUNTER BOX. Walnut; hinged lids for each of five separate parts; marks indicate it may have had labels for contents or sizes; 13¾"L x 3"W x 1¾"D.

SILVER BOX. ca: 1800s. Pine, natural finish, iron handle and latches, used a padlock now gone; dovetailed corners with top corners iron reinforced; inside compartments have lift-out trays.

TRAVEL TRUNK. All original of pine, iron bound, inside tray, (key missing) and a cloth strap holds lid upright on its brass hinges.

COWHIDE TRUNK. ca: 1700s to early 1800s. Brass head nails on iron straps and slightly domed top with brass carrier; iron lock, key gone; completely lined with original early American Arithmetic Tables papers; deep inside storage; 16″L x 8″W. Two views.

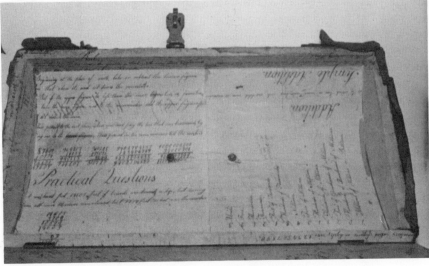

TRAVEL BOX. ca: 1700s to early 1800s. Worn leather box and handle; cotton webbing straps held lift-off lid; from a museum display.

TRUNK. Travelers' Dome Top. ca: latter 1800s into early 1900s. Heavy tin; wood strips with fancy metal ends; two snap-over catches and iron lock; inside lift-out shallow tray; leather handle replacements each side; 34″W x 24″H x 18″D.

CANDLEMOLDS. ca: 1860 - the 12-Tube, 11″H. ca: 1840 - the 4-Tube 10½″H, less often seen. Both were tinner-made with lapped edges; lucky to find these without rusted-through holes except for the only legitimate open round tops and tiny base points for wicks to protrude. Candlemolds for six to twenty-four candles were used by housewives after ca: 1750, the large (many of pewter in wood frames) scarcer and much more expensive.

CANDLE DRYING RACK. Seen in Middle Tennessee, hand-cut late in the 1880s; arms are mortised at center, held by a carved knob which is a continuation of the center pole, the pole stuck at base into a round hole in the heavy slab. Candles advanced from rushes, cording, etc. dipped in fat or pitch. Used by Europeans of the Middle Ages, the rich had wax candles, the poor had tallow. Twisted cord wicks were replaced about 1825 with plaited versions.

CANDLE BOX. ca: 1840-1850. Wall hung; hand-cut pine with slant front; much sought by collectors, these blend nicely with almost any type decor; about 16″H.

CANDLEHOLDERS. Iron wrought in Austria and treasured in America by inheriting family for a long time; has grip plates; typical hearts swing from graceful scrolls; 11½″H, base dia. 5½″.

PUSH-UP CANDLESTICKS. Brass over a hundred years old; unscrewing into two parts at deep saucer base; push-ups held in desired position with loosening or tightening of side screw-knobs; 10″H x 6″ base dia. and very heavy.

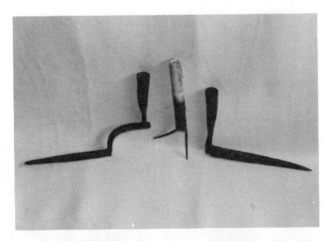

CANDLESPIKES. Very early wrought iron with candle sockets (nozzles) at one end; spike at other end could be moved about as needed, stuck into cabin walls. ALL ARE RARITIES.

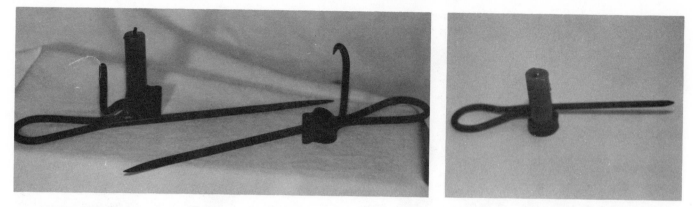

MINERS' CANDLESPIKES. (Sticking Tommys). From far Western States' mines; made on the same principle as domestic candlespikes but these were stuck into walls of mines; wrought iron with socket, spike and carrying or hanging loop. SMALLER CANDLESPIKE.

WALL LAMP. Tin with black japanned finish (hard brilliant varnish/lacquer coating); screw top to fill with kerosene; large reflector, brass burner and glass chimney.

CANDLEHOLDER. Homemade; tin with fingergrip, raised candle socket and turned-up sides.

HOGSCRAPER CANDLEHOLDER (STICK). ca: these used 1800-1850. Sharp edge of round base used to scrape hogs' bristles at butchering time; a thumb push-up; the lip fixture provides chairback hanging.

TIN LAMPS. ca: 1700s and earlier 1800s. Burned greases, whale oil and camphene. Four have saucer bases, one has a solid iron base (2nd in rear row); a handled PETTICOAT in the front stands on its own base, an improvement in 1830 over those only previously able to be hung; also in front a PUSH-UP CANDLE-HOLDER with a round fingerhold; center rear is a SINGLE WHALE OIL WICK with separate side filling tube; next is a DOUBLE FILLER with an unusually long handhold; the end WHALE OIL has a deep walled base.

CANDLEMOLDS partially seen above on the shelf.

HANGING LAMP. Pennsylvania-found antique from the late 1700s, early 1800s; largely seen on sailing ships, it hung from a ceiling hook; tight wide removable cap and a rather long filling spout; leadcoat on tin. Known since the Bronze Age, tin first came to this country on British Clipper Ships, Cornwall, England then our principal source. This artifact is indeed a rarity.

HANGING LAMP (LANTERN). Very old. Tin, handcrafted by someone for a special use; kerosene odor still clings to waste cotton wick; one side reservoir oil could flow as burned through center tube to replenish the first burner; found in New York's Northwest Ontario region; screw caps are frozen due to age and spillage buildups.

FISHING LAMP (LANTERN). Four-tube heavy sheet tin; a long wood pole fit at top middle; was fastened at the prow of a boat or held out over the water for night fishing; this type also sometimes seen at the once-so-popular street fairs and carnivals.

HANGING LAMP. All brass except 10¼" tall glass chimney; burned kerosene in last half of 1800s; marked: "Sherwoods, Ltd."; hung at the bottom of a staircase, with a hook also on the wall at the head of the stairs, so the lamp could be carried up and hung there, then taken back down as desired; base 6½" dia.

Rare MINIATURE HAND LAMPS. ca: 1700s - 1800s. Basically "limited lighting time" principle of "sparking" and tavern lamps, these evolved years apart with distinct individual characteristics. One could've been a JEWELER'S LAMP, thick emerald glass embossed at the two-mold center joint; Patented 6-14-1880; lost is the tiny chain holding a tightly fitted cap to extinguish and protect when burning, the twisted waste cotton wick. Such caps were common to these lamps since their camphene fuel was too explosive for the flame to be blown out. The fixtures are dulled brass; footed separate cup permitted the glass to be turned any way desired without falling over or spilling; 5½"H x 3½" dia.

The much earlier tinner-made LAMP, 2" square 5½"H, with tiny pull rings on raise-and-lower panels sheltering glass front and sides, has a solid back door held with a bent over tin crude latch; inside is fastened a tin snipped-out round reflector to increase the light from sperm oil fuel (originally stored in a small removable reservoir with a single cotton wick - both now missing and candle-replaced). The top ventilating forms are unique and the three-sectioned handle which can be folded flat against the lamp is undoubtedly one of the very few ever made.

WALL LAMP. Traces of green paint with rust blemishes on tin reflector; 3½" dia. olive glass blown in a mold overhangs ½", with 2½" dia. at base; brass burner unscrews to fill with oil. Lamps were not generally used until the 1800s; whale oil was available early in that century and more often used in dwellings close to seaports. Though surface rock oil (petroleum) had been known for ages, whale oil was not displaced with the advent of kerosene until after ca: 1860.

CAMPHENE LAMP. Double wick with chain-held caps.

KETTLE LAMP. Wishbone pivots on wood base to hold swinging metal oil font.

Both of New England origin in the 1700s. (Rarities).

MINIATURE LAMPS. Both follow the general size and pattern of these little lamps called by so many names, "Courting" for one, or "Tavern Night Lights", the single wick giving just enough light for as long as the suitor was permitted to visit and in taverns burned long enough for a guest to get into bed; these both oil burning. NUTMEG embossed on pressed glass; brass burner and squeeze-release brass handles holder and carrying rings; 6½"H.

Unusual MINIATURE with brass burner and reservoir; floral patterned cast-iron base; blown glass original chimney resembles flames; without chimney 6¾"H.

LACEMAKER'S or DRESS-MAKER'S LAMP. ca: 1800s. Found in Savannah, Georgia. Polished brass base, glass chimney, cranberry shade, handles and tiny round brass feet; burned kerosene - wickholder fixtures complete; 16"H.

BROODER LAMPS. Small kerosene heaters, the center galvanized tin, those at each side red painted, used to warm brooder boxes; an Iowa farmer said they used to put the lamps up on bricks to avoid setting fire to straw forming the chicks' beds; single plaited cotton wicks; they never had chimneys; brass fixtures, one top showing inside petal-like teeth which let the lamp breathe; raised name on wick keys: "The Miller Co. Made in U.S.A."; center 7¼" dia. overall 5"H, the ends each 6" dia. 4"H.

BENCH. Three-board pine cut on a homeplace in New England two centuries ago; unusually wide apron each side; bracket feet; center hand-hold cut-out and a knothole whose center long since dropped out.

BEMIS double-woven seamless COTTON BAG underneath.

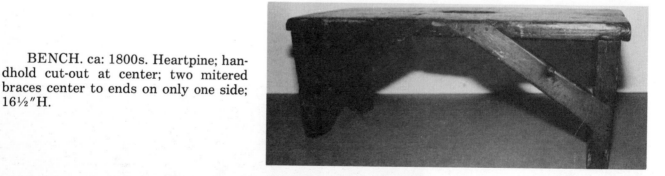

BENCH. ca: 1800s. Hand-fashioned from native pine in Vermont; still strong enough to hold considerable weight; one side legs splayed slightly more than the other side; reinforced below rounded corners, one board 10″W top; 21″L x 10″H; has a convenient lower shelf.

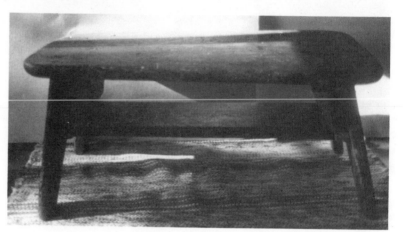

BENCH. ca: 1800s. Heartpine; handhold cut-out at center; two mitered braces center to ends on only one side; 16½″H.

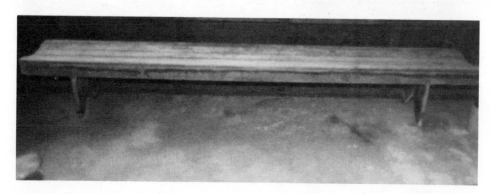

BENCH. Old; three-board top, bracket feet; dished-seat center and traces of original green paint; 16″H x 112″L x 14½″W.

DEACONS' BENCH. ca: early 1800s. Turned and grooved center spindle, 12 plain rounds each side; two plain at ends; larger turned spindles each rear corner; arms curve down into seat thought to be Pennsylvania style; 96″L x 14″W x 31¼″H.

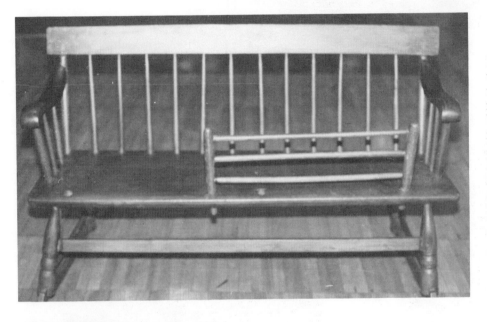

MAMMY BENCH. ca: 1820-1835. Pine, Windsor variation with 12 spindles instead of the more customary uneven number; now universally called by this name, it was first a Rocking Settee, Cradle Rocker, even Mammy Chair, the "Mammy Bench" most prevalent in the South. Baby was laid behind the gate, Mammy or Mother could rock as her hands busied themselves sewing, stringing beans, etc. With the gate removed, it became a practical family settee.

GRAIN BIN. ca: 1800s. Slant top, fastened with square nails, original red paint; 32″H x 35″W x 25″; lift top; narrow shelf at back.

MEAL BIN. ca: 1800s. Pine, four-board bin and separate piece fancy-cut base, all dovetailed corners; one-board hinged lift top; could be locked but key is missing; two divided compartments inside; 37″H x 24″W.

MEAL AND FLOUR BIN. ca: 1820-1830. Pine; origin a small town's General Store in central Illinois; iron fixtures; self knobs; two one-board-each doors were slant-pulled out and down, an inside shelf in each for one pound and other sized scoops; one-board 16"W top with low three sides gallery; 65"L x 30"H; today provides a low dining room server.

MEAL BIN. ca: 1800s. Pine, iron fixtures; uncommon slant lid opens at both front and back to provide rolling boards; two small drawers have dovetailed corners; groove trim stiles; china casters and wood handle.

MEAL BIN. ca: latter 1800s. Florida pine; one-piece sides each end in bracket feet; two separate lids for divided inside compartments raised with iron catches; iron hinges and the usual rat hole which here looks like he was a determined critter of some size; 36"L x 17¼"W and 28"H.

CHAIRS. ca: 1800s. For many years in a south Florida home. Of English oak, resembling American walnut, with burl seats; burl, the knotty outgrowth on sides of hard and semi-hardwoods, much favored by early woodworkers. Seen, for instance, on birch, ash and walnut.

ARMCHAIR was first used in an English Pub; 50"H, seat 11" x 17".

CHILD'S CHAIR. 19½" x 19".

ARMCHAIR. ca: 1800s. Low seat, finish worn off in spots; squared tapered legs, modified outcurved arms, winged back sides protecting against the chill; unusual heavy wood cord-woven back with smaller cording used for the seat weaving; brought to Tennessee by a Scottish-American. (This combination of lines was made in the Orkney Islands, a rich rural county of Scotland in the North Sea.).

ARMCHAIR. ca: 1800s. Walnut; original rush seat; note shaping of the flat spindles extending from the wider-than-usual top rail the full length of the back to the low stretcher; 34"H; seat 18"W at front narrowing at back, 13½"D.

GRANNY
ROCKER. ca: 1800s.
Hickory and hard
maple; note exten-
sion of rockers at
the back; flattened
arrowback spind-
les; an Ohio piece.

FIDDLEBACK
ROCKER. ca:
1800s. Hard
maple with a
softer wood seat as
pine or ash; original
black paint and
stenciled flowers;
extended rear
rockers.

SLATBACK
ROCKER. ca:
1800s. Mid-
western origin;
note uneven and
differences in
shaping of slats
and the small
finials; rush seat,
socketed legs with
rear extended
rockers.

BOSTON ROCKER. ca: 1830-1840.
Original black paint on hard wood with pine
seat; red and gold paint and stenciling; socketed
legs in rockers rear-extended; the first rockers
were equal distance from front and rear legs;
made in various parts of the country, but these
types were always referred to as "BOSTON".

SLATBACK CHAIR. ca: early 1800s. Note hand-cutting variations in slats and finials; hard maple; seat newly rewoven; a type used for churning, even set in the wagon bed for extra seating; could be hung on nails or hooks near the ceiling when not in use.

LADDER (SLAT) BACK CHAIR. ca: 1800s. Note uneven handcutting of slats and tiny flat finials; uncommon wood seat for this type chair; only the front stretcher is pattern-turned.

SLATBACK CHAIR. Solid cherry; note the shallow-notched donkey ears stiles' tops; chair dating from the mid to latter 1800s, the needlework was put on over original caning about the turn of the century; seat 15½″ D x 16¾″W at front, 17½″ from floor.

CLOSER VIEW of Pineapple carving on chairback.

SHAKER CHAIRS. ca: mid-1800s. Both chairs are hand-cut and lathe-turned from maple wood. Shaker furniture related to the way those in the communal groups lived (from Maine to Ohio by around 1865), purely and with simplicity; their furniture goals were always perfection of line and functionalism. Their creativity is of vast importance in our heritage, being a truly American form. And as more and more folks realize and appreciate it's impact, Shaker furniture is eagerly sought.

HIGH CHAIR. Could be pulled up to table; never had a tray; two front legs going up to secure armrest fronts are base splayed for extra rigidity against a "Youngun's scrooching around"; seat replaced.

SIDE CHAIR. ca: 1800s. All original as hand-fashioned; when the earlier one-slat backs were regarded as too uncomfortable, they were replaced with two-slats; here the piece seems worn a bit thin from so many years supporting so many leaning backs.

BLANKET CHEST. ca: 1800s. Pine six-board with lift-top on hinges; dovetailed corners; small opening near top inside box where pine cones were kept to discourage moths; New England origin; 36"W x 18½"D.

APOTHECARY CHEST. ca: 1800s. Combined woods with maple; twenty separate drawers with china pulls; 50"W.

CABINET (CLOSED CUPBOARD). ca: 1800s. Walnut; bubbles in blown glass, self-knobs, two shelves inside lower doors; two small bottom drawers have dovetailed corners; finger-roll cornice is typical of fine quality furniture; refinished to original.

SUGAR CHEST. ca: prior to 1870 when bulk sugar began to be widely sold in stores. Cherry; tapered squared legs; Middle Tennessee origin; lift-top and large self-knobs; 40"H x 18"D.

SUGAR CHEST. ca: 1820-1830. Popular in the Southland, usually kept locked in the dining room, handy at mealtimes; cherry wood; bin is set back from base drawer where tea and spices were habitually stored; sugar was kept in the two divided inside compartments under the lift-lid; 34¾"H x 30"W x 17¾"D.

CORNER CUPBOARD. ca: 1700s. North Carolina origin; three shelves above and two below (with traditional portal instigated by rats and/or mice); hand-fashioned with random width boards back (probably right "from the place"); new china knobs; 83"H x 46"W.

JELLY CUPBOARD. ca: 1800s. Walnut, white china pulls, front-grooved dovetailed corner drawers; two doors conceal inside shelves; one-board top; fancy-cut galleried top and sides; sitting flat on the floor instead of, as here, on short feet extensions of the stiles (upright corners columns), these were often known as JAM CUPBOARDS.

BEATEN BISCUIT BOARD. ca: 1800s. Kentucky origin; lift-off marble slab on poplar table with separate wood cover; seen at a museum.

JELLY CUPBOARD. ca: 1850-1860. Maryland cherry; self drawer pulls; two inside shelves; all original; 41″H x 37″W x 17″D; gallery 6″H.

JELLY CUPBOARD. ca: 1800s. Owner termed a "Backyard Project"; original paint has been stripped and piece refinished to natural wood, but fortunately, traces of the old casein base white paint still cling to the wood pores; four inside shelves and one in recessed top; random width boards for the back; 59½″H x 23¾″W x 12½″D.

STEPBACK CUPBOARD (Show and Storage). ca: 1800s. Virginia pine; brass drawer pulls; two inside shelves back of chamfered doors; grooved cornice; hand-made (means having used hand tools); 53"W x 37½"H x 18"D base of chest; partitioned top 42"H.

On top of cupboard: MELON BASKET; 6¾"H mouth 11½" x 12".

BUTTOCKS BASKET. 7"H x 9½"L.

STONEWARE CROCK (Sealing Wax). Clear glaze over yellow clay.

CORNER HANGING CUPBOARD. ca: 1800s. Pine; three shelves inside and cornice edges another on the outside top; iron latch, no key; about 26"H x 20"W.

CORNER DRY SINK. ca: 1700s. Pine; four pieces zinc bowback joined with 23"W top liner; made in Redbud, Illinois, with metal casters set in some time later to facilitate moving about; in its first home a small corner cupboard hung above; 32½"H overall.

Cast iron COOKING KETTLE with bail and pour-tilting ring.

HANGING CUPBOARD. ca: 1880-1890. Pine; three inside shelves; cornice forms another at top outside; trimmed door panel frame; no key.

PIE SAFE/CUPBOARD. ca: 1800s. Poplar with quality framed tin patterned top doors, plain panel doors below; self knobs, one long drawer; inside shelves; 80″H.

STICK STOOL. ca: 1800s. Poplar; had to be patched and the wood stained at that corner did not "take" to blend with the rest.

CHILD'S PULL-UP (YOUTH) CHAIR. ca: 1800s. Firehouse Windsor with ring turnings on two splayed (for rigidity) front legs and splayed (for comfort) back spindles; two back legs and stretchers are plain rounds; hard maple; never had a tray; eye-caned original seat was tattered and replaced with padding preparatory to getting a new cloth covering. Seat 12″ x 11″.

BOX. ca: 1800s. Pine, iron latch and side handles; an individual could have made it for his tools but it was found in a cabin holding quilts and prized needlework.

WOOD BOX. Seen in Florida; pine with softly faded original blue paint; 24"H x 22"W x 20"D.

CRADLE. ca: 1800s. Five-board dovetailed four corners poplar; handgrip cut-outs each end; 39"L x 15½"W.

CRADLE. ca: 1700s. Basic patterns of rocking cradles have changed very little since the 1300s; Pilgrims liked rectangular panels, later innovations included finials only for appearance, then various hoods, canopy posts, side spindles and so on. But no cradle was ever quickly disposed of, usually remaining in one family for several generations of rocking. This one was handcrafted in Pennsylvania more than a hundred and fifty years ago, retaining to a fine degree its original mustard yellow paint; iron fixtures.

MINIATURE BONNET CRADLE.

Ca: 1700s. Hand-crafted of thinly shaved walnut. Bentwood bonnet, white painted inside with gold band outside; 6"L x 2¼"W.

CHILDREN'S TABLE. ca: 1800s. From the estate sale of a relative of the founder of Larkin Furniture Co., Buffalo, N.Y.; quarter cut oak top and apron, maple legs; has an extra 3½"W leaf fitting into the sides-pulled-out center with wood pegs; 18¾"H overall. 3"D apron sides; top 23½" square.

CHILDREN'S STAKE WAGON. ca: 1800s. Type of farm wagon; all wood with iron fixtures and iron bound wheels, the larger in the rear; a wood pulling tongue (here detached due to limited wall space).

GOAT WAGON. ca: 1800s. Hand-fashioned of wood and iron; complete and ready for harnessing a small animal to pull the children.

CHILD'S DRESSER-CHEST. ca: 1800s. Walnut with light maple drawer fronts; china knobs; square nails; 4'H x 22"W x 15"D. (Rare).

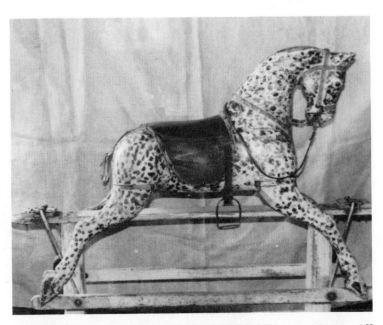

ROCKING HORSE (HOBBYHORSE). ca: 1800s. All original in excellent condition with good paint, leather saddle and harness and metal stirrups; rocks back and forth on a simple arrangement of iron and wood fixtures; seen in Michigan.

SLED. ca: 1700s to 1800s. Massachusetts hand-fashioned of wood and iron; one runner; handholds under each seat end; a style known late in the 18th century.

YOUTH CHAIR. ca: early 1800s. Walnut pull-up-to-table; never had a tray; pine seat 12½″ x 11″; 5″W (age-split) footrest; overall 33¼″H, Southern Illinois origin - handmade.

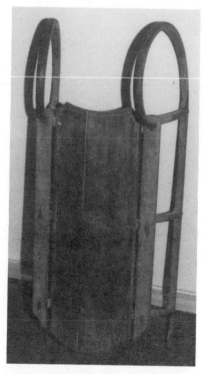

SLED. ca: 1800s. Wood and iron with curved front runners; New England origin; traces of original red and yellow paints.

SLED. ca: 1800s. Maryland origin; all original; mixed woods hand-crafted with red, yellow and faded green paints; iron bound runners; posts mortised securely into three-slats seat with wider boards at sides; 28″L x 13″W, seat 9″H, backrail 9″H.

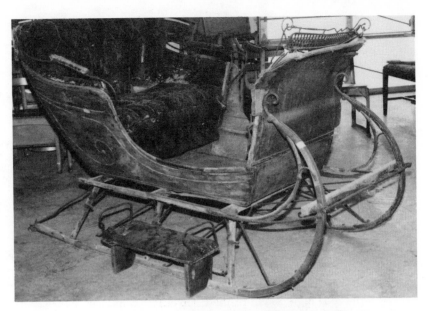

SLEIGH. ca: 1800s. Wood with iron fixtures; the whole badly in need of restoring including button-tufted velour type upholstering; carries a folding STOOL, BUGGY WHIP HOLDER and SNOW SHIELD (which used separately would make a decorative piece).

BATHING TUB. ca: 1800s. Tin; used at an Inn restored at an Indiana museum; seat allowed feet to rest in well; filled from buckets and tilt-emptied through open tube under seat.

SLANT TOP DESK. ca: 1700s. Pine; iron keeper, can be locked; 3"H top back and short sides gallery as well as a narrow one around front and sides of the slant top; 41"H x 29½"W x 28½"D. (Flathead primitively carved DUCK DECOY on box underneath).

SHELF. ca: 1840-50. Pine; two shelves mortised together with shaped sides; 34½"L x 12½"D.

Pewter metric measuring TANKARDS kept on shelf with illegible hallmarks and quantities on squared handles.

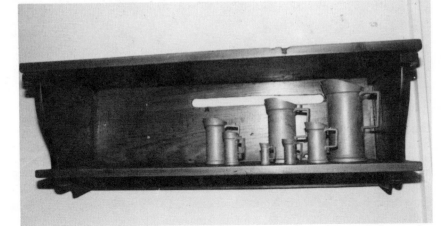

MILKING STOOL (Above). ca: 1800s. Virginia pine; three splayed legs slash-pinned through seat for extra strength; (right) kindlin' was sometimes chopped on the underside; 12"H x 12"W x 9"D one end of thick seat, 7½" the other.

STOOL. ca: 1800s. Pine; deep scalloped apron; crooked bracket feet; 19½"L x 7½"W.

MILKING STOOLS. ca: 1800s. Two at ends have legs cut through the seats, slashed and wood pinned (pegged) in the customary old way; Southern Indiana farm origin. Hickory slab 2½" thick on three natural branch legs; half-moon cut hickory; bark stripped natural branch legs irregularly splayed; center is finely finished hard maple with a dished-center seat; sides are grooves trimmed. It reminded an Austrian-American family of their Alpine homeland; 15"H x 14" dia. x 3½" thick seat.

Two hickory slabs held together with short splayed legs; farm made; still not wobbly.

FOOTSTOOL. ca: 1800s. Walnut; square nails; one slightly bent bracket foot; holes on side indicate a cover (needlework, for instance) may have been there originally; refinished; these little "cricket stools" kept the feet off drafty floors.

CLOSE-UP of carved top.

MILKING STOOL (Left). ca: 1850. Farm handmade; one leg replaced - crudely nailed on at one side; top is 1½" thick. ORNAMENTAL STOOL (Right). ca: 1800s. Hand-cut with three splayed legs; 10" dia. top has been carved into oak leaves with initials "SM" entwined at center; 13"H.

BEDSTOOL. ca: 1800-1840. Pennsylvania origin; combined woods.

TRESTLE TABLE. ca: 1800s. Refinished oak, arched base pedestal; 29½"H x 88"L x 31½W.

DROPLEAF TABLE. ca: 1800s. Pine; when the table was refinished, the end board (of another tree) came out lighter, as though it had been painted; one-board 20"W top x 28½"H; drop leaves each 14"W x 41½"L.

COUNTRY TABLE. ca: 1800s. Walnut; one-board top; all original with normal wear marks, including ink stains on top; spool-turned legs; drawer with flat self knobs is four-corner dovetailed; 29¾"H x 26¼"W x 70"L.

COUNTER TABLE. Chestnut with turned maple legs; 20″W with hinged dropleaves down, 42″W with leaves both up; origin Wilson, N.Y.; 47″L x 29¼″H.

DINING TABLE. ca: 1840. One-board top pine; silver drawer one side with porcelain knob; 70″L x 32¾″W x 32″H.

TABLE. ca: 1800s-1900. Salesman's sample; walnut with one-board poplar top; turned legs on which present owner added metal floor shields; 19¼″H x 16″W x 10½″D.

TABLE/STAND. ca: 1800s. Plain; pine with squared tapered legs, one slightly warped.

TABLE (Sometimes called Parlor). ca: first quarter 1800s. Five-board construction with two dovetailed drawers; dull brass pulls; Virginia origin. 29″H x 21½″ square top.

TABLE. ca: 1840. Walnut with one-board top; turned legs; one-drawer dovetailed corners with dull brass knob; 28½″H; top 23″ x 22½″. The VEGETABLE BASKET here holding magazines dates about 1880. The milk glass KEROSENE LAMP. ca: 1880.

TABLE. ca: 1800s. Pennsylvania origin; from walnut on the homeplace; used three pieces to eke out the top; nicely scalloped apron four sides; 14″ x 11½″ and 18″H.

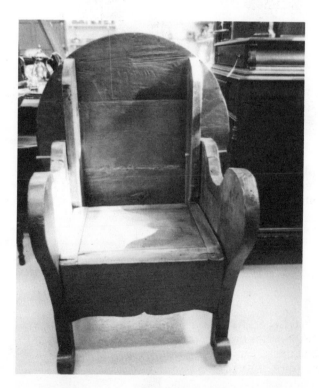

CHAIR TABLE or TABLE CHAIRS have been made since the 1600s, pushed back against walls for convenience, and the table keeping drafts off the person seated; a Florida east coast dealer said beyond buying it because she liked it and "felt" it was old, she only knew it had been hand-fashioned of pine in Alabama. An example of the maker's interpretation of various styles, the seat is lift-top for an invalid's convenience; the table is a useful surface. Table 29½″ dia. x 1¾″ thick; seat 16¼″D x 18″W. Different.

BOOKS. Pub. 1803. THE FARMER'S BOY. A rural poem by Robert Bloomfield, New York; Printed by Hopkins & Seymour; Sold by G.F. Hopkins No. 118 Pearl Street.

Pub. 1889. THE LONDON MEDICAL STUDENT by John R. Alden, Publisher, New York.

Pub. 1850. THE CONVICT SHIP by Colin A. Browning, M.D.

Pub. 1854. THE WORKING MAN'S SUNDAY . . . HOW TO SPEND IT . . . Help for the Working Man.

Pub. 1906. PRICE'S MEMORANDUM ACCOUNT BOOK. Designed for Farmers, Mechanics and All People.

HOUSE BELL. ca: 1800s. Kept outside on the wall of a covered entry; visitors pulled the cord to announce arrival; brass with iron clapper mounted on ornately fashioned and decorated wood. Owner brought many years ago from Germany, purchased there as an old piece. 31"H x 9"W.

DOLL'S DRESS. ca: 1870. Red wool dress handmade by a Pittsburg, Pennsylvania dressmaker, completely lined with buckram to stiffen; moss green velvet at the beadedge revers, and it also holds white lace at wrists and neckline, further trimming about 1" above the underhem; full caps drape the shoulders; tiny hooks and eyes form the back closing halfway down the skirt.

CHILD'S SHOES. ca: 1800s to 1900. Complete six buttons, leather, lightly worn soles. Pioneer children would've been excited at these, handling them gingerly, never dreaming they'd own such a pair. A caring frontier father would somehow find time to hunt, and then tack an animal's skin to dry on the outside wall of their cabin, next scrape to soften. "Dressing" it for better pliability, with a knife and a precious iron shoelast (if he had one) he'd cut and shape crude shoes and boots for his family, often using chestnut pegs to hold the soles. Shoes were saved for Sunday-wearing to Meetings, but always slipped off upon reentering the home. Shoelasts were handed down (as were shoes if they lasted that long), many Granddads into the 1920s still using them for home shoe repairs as folks had always done.

FLUE COVER. ca: 1800s. Placed over a wall opening which in winter held the top end of a wood or coal burner's stovepipe; in summer while the stove was being cleaned, it was a decorative cover for the gaping hole in a wall; gold, black and subdued work clothes' colors with a brass frame and chain; metal; 6¼" dia. Now being heavily reproduced with all sorts of pictures.

MIRROR with HAT and COAT RACK. ca: 1875-1880. Overall 40" x 36"; for many years hung on a river paddleboat out of St. Louis, Missouri; shaped like a ship's wheel; mirror walnut framed; missing is a porcelain ball and one is a replacement; lacking is one spoke's finial.

FRAKTUR . . . BIRTH and BAPTISMAL RECORD. All original; handblown glass and gold lined walnut frame with carved leaves; brass-ringed porcelain dots at each corner; Fraktur itself 11¼" x 15½". Still vivid brushwork in watercolors and flowing penstrokes (resembling a type of calligraphy stemming from ancient Arabic Crusades, a method also seen on many deeds of German, English, Swiss and other immigrants obtaining land here). The Pastor holds the baby at the font; well dressed in period garments are two ladies in floor-length dresses, and two men, the head of a third visible over a shoulder, along with Biblical figures and verses, kneeling children, a cross and anchor, doves, chalice, flowers, vine traceries and more. All is in the German language as customary in Teutonic settlements on our Niagara Frontier and elsewhere in America. The official portion translates: "To Partners Henry Clay and his wedded housewife Friednicke born Lindhorst, to these two people was born on the 3rd of January in the year of our Lord 1872 in Town Lewistown, Niagara County, New York, and on the 28th of January 1872 before the aforementioned (undersigned) was baptized in the name of Maria Wilhelmina Johanna. The Godparents were Mrs. Karl Woeker and Mrs. Karl Moehl and Mr. Joh. Lindhorst. Witness was Joh. Wilhelm Weinbach who is the Pastor of St. Patri Congregation, Town Cambria, Niagara County, New York."

"CHICKS". Printed on cotton and signed "Schwab & Wolf, N.Y. Made in U.S.A. Copyright 1899 U.S."; 22¾" square; blending soft background farm tones for a blonde child wearing a ruby red velvet dress over a white lace petticoat, holding a chick in her hand, while her sunbonnet has fallen back off her head; features are doll-like perfect; (for many, many years, particularly in porcelains, dolls were used as models because of their beauty).

HAIRWORK. ca: 1800s. Human hair of a deceased member of a family in shades of brown woven around a wire base into a wreath of florals and bowknots and framed for remembrance. Mourning customs for dress and social behavior were rigidly imposed, beginning in the early 1700s, fading about the 1880s. Human hair, even children's, was twisted and woven into various prized jewelry items, rings, lockets, pins, etc. in the form of butterflies, flowers, even portraits and given also for remembrance and/or love tokens.

SAMPLER . . . AMERICAN FOLK ART. An 18th century example of a type of cross stitching, using hand dyed floss on hand-woven linen (framed in a more modern day); white, brown, mustard yellow and greens are softly faded; there are tasseled draperies, the roof of a distant house, a bird, cloud, flowers, center urn or fountain; (fancier stitchery began around 1800, expanding farm scenes, eagles, farm animals and children, for instance); numbers are from one to ten; both capital and small letters of the alphabet - but no "J" in either case; pious verses were used more often than not: "Mary Lord, her Sampler, was wrought September 25, 1792, age 11 years; born December the 9, 1781; God loveth the child whose words are mild" - and - "There is an hour when I must die, Nor do I know how soon Twill come, a Thousand Children young as I, are Called by death to hear Their doom". Learning ordinary sewing was imperative in settlement days and much later; samplers were a way in which young women and small girls could learn to read and write; 10⅛" x 11⅛".

OFFERINGS BASKET. ca: 1800s. Silk tasseled black velvet pouch on a substantial brass ring, two wood handles remaining from original three; elders standing in the aisles passed baskets down pews or benches in a mid-Tennessee church.

OFFERINGS BASKET. A wire strainer cup, inside lined with felt, rolled over edge; probably handstitched by a member of the church; wood handle.

SADDLEBAGS. From early pioneer days well into the 1900s these brass-studded double-sewn leather pouches held mail for horseback (or mule) delivery into country districts of Tennessee's Cumberland Plateau region, one bag hanging either side of the animal's back. The bags could be slung over the arm or grasped by the handle to tote, used by U.S. Cavalry units, frontiersmen, itinerant preachers, wherever needed to hold smaller travel items. In April 1860, a western freighting line began our colorful PONY EXPRESS, using saddlebags for their approximate two hundred riders to carry mail about 2,000 miles from St. Joseph, Missouri to Sacramento, California in eight to ten days, changing mounts at swing stations about 15 miles apart, ever in imminent peril from hostiles (Indians). Told not to stand and fight, they were to get away in a hurry - hopefully outdistancing their howling pursuers! Once telegraph lines became satisfactorily operable, Pony Runs ceased.

HOTEL (INN) WASHSTAND SET. Missouri origin. ca: 1800s. Wireware stand with replacement wood shelf set in a groove; side towel bars; 30″H.

TRAY. ca: 1800s. From a southwestern frontier saloon; brass-collared eye ring on one end for hanging; impressed date "Pat. July 8, 1887"; thinly rolled sheetiron galvanized; 26″L x 19″W; handsome in a wall grouping of collectibles.

BEDWARMERS. ca: 1800s. Once used in a German inn, found with a family in Canada; light brown glaze stoneware; brass screw tops and rings; very heavy even without being filled with hot water.

From a mid-central Kansas town in the 1800s. HOTEL KEY RACK (Top), wall hung. Wood, having 56 niches with paper labels of room numbers; keys were laid on the individual shelves, handy behind the clerk's desk. (Rare). HOTEL ROPE BOX (Bottom). One placed in each room in case of dangers - as fire - with a strong length of rope laid in this heavy tin hinged lid box; for easy removal, the rope unfolded without knotting. One end was fastened to a windowside hook and the room occupant slid down to safety. (Rare).

TEAPOT. Probably used at an Inn dining room; commercial; brown glazed stoneware inside and out; originally had a spigot (cork in now) and lid is a replacement; about 10″ dia. widest part, 9″H.

TEAPOT. Advertising words are dot-etched HARPER COLD TEA; finial is a flower; Taunton quadruple plate from the 1870s; 5¼″ widest part, 3¾″H without finial.

WALL LAMP. ca: 1800s. In 1867, George M. Pullman, a cabinetmaker, after converting old railroad coaches into sleeping cars to better facilitate long distance travel, "extra fare for extra-fine comfortable furnishings", founded the successful Pullman Palace Car Co. This LAMP dated 1871 impressed: "Made for L&N RR by the Adams & Westlake Co., Chicago, Illinois" was set out 9½″ from the car wall when installed. It has the original hand-painted shade, three brass base sections lightly etched in a pretty pattern, tiny round brass candlewick and kerosene burner fixtures. Impressed on the unusual burner is: "H.G. Moehring"; full width 8″, 8½″H.

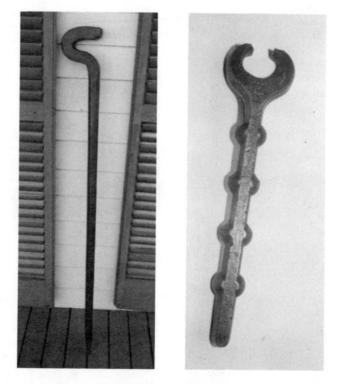

Two RAILROAD WRENCHES (Left). The heavier 38″L. ca: 1800s. (Right) The shorter about 12″L has an "H" in a shield on the pincers and marked for the "ATSF Ry".

RAILROAD PULLMAN CAR LAVATORY. ca: latter 1800s. Wall mounted; wood with porcelain bowl; shell design seen when the piece is closed has traces of gilt paint; tin soap case and toothbrush holder with pushdown water spigot; heavy iron rod fold-up legs.

TRAMP ART. Several generations ago a tramp arrived at a midwestern rural home asking for a meal handout. Instead, he remained all winter, paying for his keep by penknife (pocketknife) chip-carving the center of this walnut newel post (not for sale, of course, but very expensive if purchasable). A step from the early casual "kindlin'-stick whittlin'", this type work could be called "The Vagrants' Trademark." Soft woods as cigar boxes and crates, whatever was at hand, were used, the finished articles then stained, painted, even gilded. They were carved by wanderers who "rode the rails", dropping off freight cars when trains slowed down at farms and smaller hamlets to bum a meal, and a bed in stormy weather, barnloft hay being warm and dry. Occasionally, one tried to sell or barter something already completed, others were willing to do chores, even hard field work. In those years it was not uncommon to see a Hobo sitting in the shade near a kitchen door hungrily shoveling vittles into his mouth from, hopefully, a heaped-up plate. And where lived a particularly generous housewife, the man trudged away with an additional sack of thick sandwiches and apples, which he'd try to stuff into his raggedy jacket pocket. (Sometimes his tentative knock ended with the dogs being "set on him" and then he'd skedaddle in a hurry.) When a tramp remained to work, in spare time he'd often carve a gift for the family, many now coming to popular notice. Perishable, and not always expertly carved, sometimes not really appreciated, much was thrown away, but fine pieces are attractive and ascending in value.

TRAMP ART TOY DRESSER. (Left) Carefully detailed chip-carved walnut and cigar box woods, designs on the self knobs of the pullout drawer; tilting mirror. Close-up of drawer interior (above) has original cigar box label colorfully intact; 10″ widest part, 5″D x 13½″H.

TRAMP ART PICTURE FRAME. ca: 1890-1900. Stained and sparsely gilt on rare walnut; four chip-carved sides; separate squares and curved corners are glued on a 1¼″W x ¾″D solid walnut backing frame; overall 15½″ square; individual chip carving differences evident in this handwork.

BARBER SHOP POLE. Massachusetts origin; early hand-cut; faded red, white and blue original paint; 22″H x 7″W.

OCCUPATIONAL SHAVING MUG. ca: 1880, Michigan origin. About 1840 soap was packaged in mugs instead of round boxes; "exclusive" shops kept these for their customers between barbering visits, the mugs marked only with initials and/or numbers. Universally after 1865, shops kept mugs stashed in cubbyhole cabinets, the containers painted with individual names, trades, hobbies, favorite sports, etc. Shaving brushes were also kept with the bar inside and when ready for use, the water-dipped brush could activate suds from the soap. This belonged to a tavern owner, his name in gilt and business picture in bright colors. Mug is 3¾″ dia. x 3¾″H.

CIGAR MOLD.
For twenty; wood two
sections pin-fastened
together; 22″L x
5¼″W.

CIGAR MOLD. ca: 1800s. Cigar in top section might have been a "fun" piece; at least one Tennessee father gave these out at the birth of his first child. Ten-cigar wood mold; two pieces fastened with wood pin at top and bottom, pin on one side fitting into hole on other; after the dampened leaves were rolled and placed in the molds, several molds were clamped in an iron vise for compressing-shaping the cigars. (Outside wrappers were added later). 20″L x 11″W.

COOPER'S HEADER (HOOPSETTER). ca: 1800s. One-piece oak; top mashed from years of mallet strikes, setting hoops on kegs, barrels, etc.; smithy-added iron ring against splitting; underside has a middle concave groove to fit hoops' edges.

COBBLER'S STOOL. ca: 1800s. Hand-cut splay-legged stool in hickory with a cast-iron shoelast fit into seat slot. Cobblers often kept various-sized lasts for whole families.

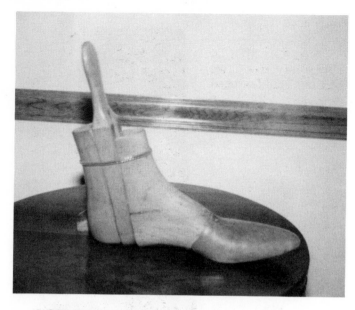

LOW BOOT MOLD. Four wood parts fit together; size "VII" incised at top; 15"H x 9¼"L foot.

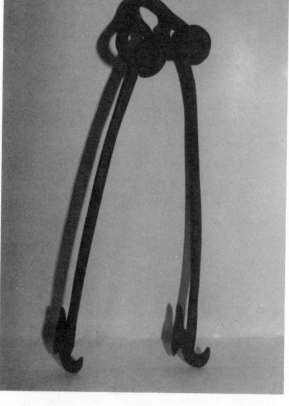

BARREL LIFTS (HOOKS). Smithy's iron work; fastened at the top to chains, it was used to raise kegs, barrels, etc. on a hoist; adjusted at the top to fit many sizes.

SOAP PADDLE. ca: 1800s. Carved wood; these used at soapmakers Proctor & Gamble, Cincinnati, Ohio; solid oak 7"L and 10"W, 1" thick; etched with an honorary message and given to an employee for a special occasion.

MILL SPOOLS. ca: 1800s. Georgia origin; dogwood, metal bound; 14"H x 2" dia.

FISHMONGER'S HORN. ca: 1800s. Japanned black finish on tin; wood mouthpiece complete with "sounder"; peddlers in animal-drawn wagons went up and down (coastal) cities' streets in the early morning to peddle freshly caught seafoods; about 14″L.

HORSE'S HEAD. Repaint date on back "1898". Found in the attic during renovation of St. Augustine, Florida Y.M.C.A.; 18½″ x 14½″.

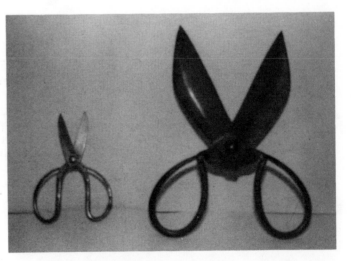

TINNER'S SHEARS. ca: 1800s into 1900s. Also used by coppersmiths, etc. Larger; 11¾″L.

TAILOR'S SCISSORS. ca: 1800s (could be earlier). Impressed date and smithy's touchmark unreadable.

MEN'S DRESS COAT FORM. ca: 1800s; silk over a stiffened cotton shape; solid walnut stand; once in a Men's Clothing Emporium at Murfreesboro, Tennessee.

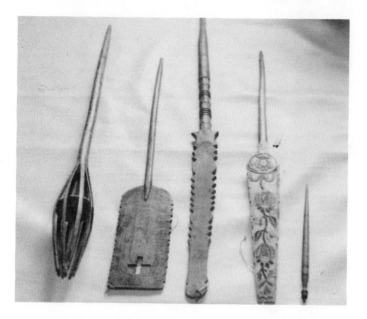

DISTAFFS (FLAX STICKS). ca: 1700s. Hand-fashioned from wood; could be made at home or by woodworkers, sometimes as special gifts, straight sticks bent to proper forms desired, some plain, others elaborately cut and carved. They held unspun flax - principally wool or tow fluffs in spinning. Four here were held underarm; the smallest a HAND-SPINDLE; the cage-type a "turned" DISTAFF; but all now rarely found.

LABEL MAKER PART. Pennsylvania factory origin; part of loom for making (silky) clothing labels; an endless loop chain ran over this piece; steel pegs fit into the loops; pegs are programmed for desired pattern; two gears run on a depressed track. 3"H x 3½"L. (These were conversation pieces seen on a Keeping Room table.)

CASTLE WHEEL. Early one; walnut. American owner believes it to be of European origin; these small wheels were called "Visiting Wheels" because they were so easy to transport.

QUILL and BOBBIN WINDER (PIRN). ca: 1700s. Hand-turned wheel device (used preparatory toward weaving cloth) to rewind spun yarn after it has been washed and perhaps dyed, measuring and removing any kinks.

WEAVER'S CHAIR (Above). ca: 1700s. Maple; used by worker seated at a loom; arms mortised through curved arm rail; low seat on natural branch splayed legs. WEAVER'S STOOL (Right). ca: 1800s. Maple; lathe-turned legs and seat; iron stretchers.

ADVERTISING: Older artifacts are, generally, of heavier gauge metal with porcelain appearing in the last of the 1800s. Fewer paper signs remain in any kind of condition since that material was less durable than wood or metals; and tin was used in all sorts of containers. About 1850 Somers Bros. of Brooklyn, New York devised a method of replacing paper labels with a type of lithographing. Any lithographed can, particularly in brilliant colors, is usually of more value with a picture on it than one with merely names and places. Subjects remain endless in collecting old advertising items.

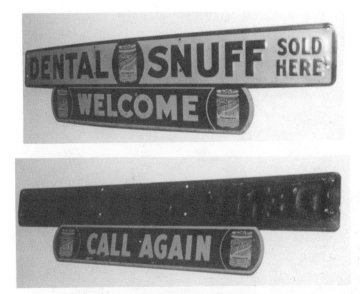

RED MAN TOBACCO SIGN. Found in North Carolina; red, yellow, black and white on tin.

DENTAL SNUFF SIGN. Enameled; embossings in white, red, yellow and black; hung at the door in a way that both incoming and outgoing customers could read it.

BIRDSELL WAGONS SIGN. Black on yellow embossing; enameling on tin.

DUCK HEAD OVERALLS SIGN. ca: Last of 1800s. Tin, recently natural wood framing; several colors with Duck's Head trademark.

DAVIS SEWING MACHINE. Paper card (newly framed in antique walnut); many soft colors for Mill, Home, Snow, Moon, etc.; printed "No Cogs, No Annoyances", and more; 3¼" x 4¼".

WIGWAM . SYRUP. Log Cabin's; glass; pouring lip on each side; white background with etched letters; restaurant style.

BOTTLES. 8½" to 10"H. All were blown in two-part molds and have demijohn (pushed up) bottoms, "bubbles" and applied tops. C.W. HERWIG CASE GIN. ca: 1890; dark green, petticoat top. J.J.W. PETERS CASE GIN. ca: 1820-1850; hot glass ran down one side when applied to the top; olive green; ¾"H; Bird Dog Trade Mark with Bird. SCHEIDAM AROMATIC SCHNAPPS. ca: 1840-1860; dark green. Same SCHEIDAM except a smaller bottle with twisted-on top. NO NAME. ca: 1800-1830; one side depressed below ⅞" top.

COOKIE (BISCUIT) TIN. Colorful with geometric designs overall; called a "LUNCH PAIL TIN" because it was so used after original contents were eaten; still has its small brass hook and latch.

FRESH SEIDLITZ POWDERS TIN. Hinged lid; yellow box with much lettering; contents were mixed with water and drunk as an effervescing salts; long ago was an important household item.

MORRIS WHITE LEAF BRAND LARD. Bright designs and lettering on tin; at butchering time the lacy outside of pork intestines known as "leaf fat" was used to start lard making in the bottom of a huge lard kettle. A hog's head was rendered out (fat extracted); this became the choice white fat saved for baking on special occasions since it was lighter and fluffier; 7¾"H x 6¾" dia.

CIGAR BOX. SAULS HAND MADE KINGS printed inside the lid and outer topside of dovetailed-corners wood box; tiny brass hook latch and keeper intact; remains of original tax stamp; 3¾"H x 7¼"W x 6"D.

TARTAR BRAND SOAP BOX.

MO-SAM COFFEE TIN. Original paper label on tin; packed in Baltimore, Maryland; beautiful scenic of Egyptian landscape with pyramids; the motto "Always the Same".

ARMOUR'S STAR PURE LARD PAIL. Tin with wire bail; eight pounds net.

BLANKE'S COFFEE. Best Value; original colorful fancy designs faded but readable; tin.

GOLDEN TWINS. Tobacco Tin; hinged lid; black on bright yellow tin.

UNION LEADER CUT PLUG TIN. Red and gold with eagles, scrolls, brass bail and side catch; 4¼"D x 7¼"W x 5⅛"L.

TIGER BRIGHT SWEET CHEWING TOBACCO TIN. P. Lorillard Co., Jersey City, N.J.; basketweave red and black with large tigers' heads; fold down flat handles and lift lid; 7¾"L x 5⅞"H x 6⅜"W.

"POCKET" TOBACCO TIN EDGEWORTH PLUG SLICE. Smoking Tobacco; Larus & Bro. Co., Richmond, Virginia, U.S.A.; 4¼"L x 3"W x 1"D.

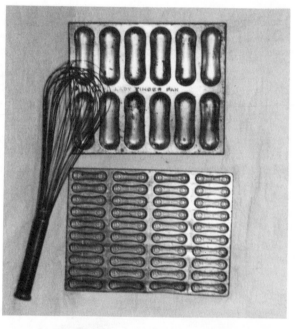

LADY FINGER PAN (Marked). Twelve sections tin.

BAKER'S WIRE WHISK. Large size; wireware with metal grip.

CHOCOLATE CANDY MOLDS. Cats' Heads at both ends of forty individual pieces.

BAKER'S FLOUR BIN. ca: 1850. Pine, refinished from original green paint to natural wood, although traces of paint still cling; hinged slant lid with china knob; narrow top makes a shelf; one-piece sides each end in bracket cut-outs.

**COOKIE ROLLER.** One-piece birds-eye maple hand-cut; New England origin.

**FOOD STOMPER.** Unusual in cherry wood; early.

**MEAL FUNNEL.** Walnut, corners dovetailed; rare; Pennsylvania origin.

**FLOUR/MEAL SIFTER.** Wrapped wood holding wire mesh and rod crisscross supports.

**CHOCOLATE MELTER.** ca: 1800s. Brass; iron handle with eye ring; owner believed this had first been a Candy Dipper, then the iron legs were added for second purpose. Bottom shows signs of heat.

**CAKE PEEL.** ca: 1700s. Smithy-made; rattail handle end provides a hanging ring; bread peels usually had longer handles; 12"L widest part tapering to about 3¼".

TWO CANDY PANS. (Above). COPPER. ca: mid-1800s; Georgia origin. 19″ Dia.; iron ring under rolled-over rim; side handles are iron.

BRASS (Left). ca: mid-1800s; Tennessee origin. About 20″ dia. flat iron ring under rim; no handles.

MEATBLOCK. ca: 1830-40. Traces of original red stain on sycamore wood; three fat turned legs; Indiana origin; about 28″H x 20″ Dia.

CUTTING BLOCK. From a Kentucky museum; cut one piece from a log, short squared legs.

HOOK. To drag hogs' carcasses to the scalding kettles; (type used as cotton bale hooks and many other uses).

MEAT CLEAVER. Butcher's tool used for chopping (cutting) meat; steel with wood over a steel handle; very old.

HOG DRAG HOOK. ca: 1800s. Blacksmith-made of wood and iron; to pull a carcass more easily in butchering.

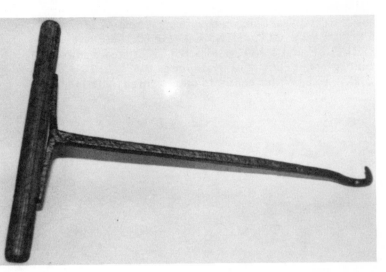

COUNTER SACK HOLDER. Wireware, nine sack shelves; carrying top; 29½"H x 9½"W base x 8½"D tapering up to 4½"W x 2½"D; fairly scarce item.

PAPER SACK RACK. Wireware on a wood wall-hanging back with beveled edges and eye ring; six graduated size holders; 36"H x 5½"W; scarce item.

PAPER SACKS for COFFEE. Paper was substituted for cotton bags and other containers during the Civil War when cotton became scarce. LUCKY POT, TWO BIT, DINNER BELL, MOBALA, GREER'S and a NO NAME BRAND; colors in red, blue, green, yellow and white, sizes 9¼"L to 13½"L, 3¼"W to 5"W; for contents one to three pounds net.

LINSEED OIL CAN in thin WOOD CASE. Galvanized tin can with grooved dome shoulders; corncob stopper, wire bail with wood grip; evidence it first had a screw top.

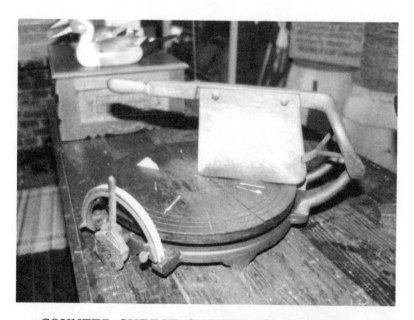

COUNTER CHEESE CUTTER. Wood and iron; hand-operated; raised metal tab on platform held cheese hoop firm; wedge sizes adjustable; blade 8" x 6½".

MILK BOTTLE.
Dated but unreadable;
looks like latter 1800s;
glass with tin frame;
spring catch holds flat
glass lid firmly.

**DELIVERY BASKETS.** Heavy sheet tin with wood side handles; edges rolled over heavy wire reinforcing.

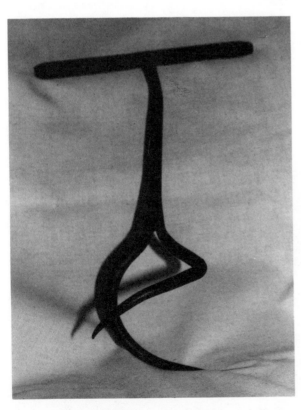

SUGAR DEVIL. ca: 1870s. Iron; two very sharp prongs; about 18″L, handle 11″W.

SUGAR DEVIL. (Above). ca: 1850. Iron 17″L, wood handle 10½″W; all generally made with same basic idea, to loosen sugar (usually brown or "basin") that became impacted when shipped in wood barrels and sold from them in the stores; while in a pinch it could also losen dried fruits so packed, the sharp pointed prongs would cut that product. This FRUIT AUGER'S teeth were better for that purpose; cast iron, Pat. Dated. May 2, 1883.

SNUFF JAR. ca: 1800s. REDWARE, dark brown metallic glaze inside and out; tightly fitting japanned tin lid; 6¼"H x 5" widest bulbous center; bottom 4" dia.

STORE SCALE (Also used at home). ca: 1800s to 1900. Cast iron basket; polished brass with iron red and yellow stenciled base; Salter Scale No. 50; Made in Holland; could weigh ten pounds by half ounces; 13"H x 9½" Dia. tin tray.

SPRING BALANCE SCALE. ca: 1800s. Pelouze Mfg. Co., Chicago, Illinois, U.S.A.; brass faced; iron, 19" hook to handle; calibrated to 100 pounds.

SCALE. Coffin-red painted iron like new with three separate weights; brass arm; tin basket.

FISHTAIL SCALE. American Cutlery Co.; iron red-painted with green and black striping; has the metal Seal of Indiana and lead sealer after test-inspection; 12½"L x 6¼"H x 7" dia. plate; wts. comp.

SCALE BASKET. Footed brass, rolled rim; sizes and prices are many and varied.

HANGING SCALE FRARY'S FAMILY BALANCE. 20 pounds; brass, iron and tin; tray 10¼" x 11½", 27"H overall. Used both in stores and homes.

SPOOL CABINET CLARK'S O.N.T. (Our New Thread); china knobs; one board top; dovetailed four corners; individual inside spool compartments; counter style; 23½"W x 17"D, about 18"H.

SPOOL COTTON THREAD CASE, WILLIMANTIC. Front, back, sides (shown) finished to be attractive from every angle when the case was set on a store counter; elaborately decorated in red, black and gilt colors with deep embossings; scrolls and scallops, fancy glass knobs with brass screws and collars; two dovetailed drawers have separate spool partitions inside; one piece wood top; 8½"H x 23½"W x 16½"D.

SPICE BIN. From a General Store at a remote crossroads in a far western state; wood held by square nails; half circle drawers have white porcelain knobs; could be set on a counter, table or hung at a handy height; thick 2½"H scalloped gallery, 15½"H overall, 9¾"W x 7½"D; a rare decorative and still useful artifact.

MINCEMEAT BUCKETS. ca: 1800s. Two, center and bottom, each have wire bails with wood grips and wrapped iron bands; that at center carries its original coffin-red paint and a lapped-ends side lid fitting down over the rim; the lower or original mustard yellow paint has a plain set-on lid; 9½" and 12½" dia.

The top of the stack SUGAR BUCKET has lapped-over wood bands brad fastened, and wrapped edges of lid held the same way; flat wood handle is missing; loose sugar absorbed any odor so odorless white pine was used insofar as possible for staves, covers and bottoms; hoops and handles were of resilient-for-bending swamp ash or hickory.

FLOUR BARREL. ca: 1800s. Cooper made, wrapped bands, staved sides, lid replaced to original; from a General Store in middle Tennessee; 30½"H x 14½" dia.

COTTAGE CHEESE DRAINER on BARREL used in a home. Hard maple, thick staved sides, iron bands; revolving top on base has holes for drainage; weight squeezed out the whey; 7¼" dia. mouth.

SHIPPING BOX. Wood; vividly colored paper labels with a buffalo head, flowers, other designs; the R. OVENS BAKERS, U.S. BAKING CO. BUFFALO, N.Y.; in today's adaptations, a low table for display and storage; the one-piece hinged lid was replaced. 23½″L x 13¾″W x 11½″H.

SHIPPING BOX. One end imprinted: "12-10-08"; wood corners dovetailed; original paper labels each side and back in brilliant blues and other colors, a man holding a bar of ACME SOAP, LAUTZ BROS. & CO.'S The Best Tar Soap Made; L.H. Spaulding, Middleport, N.Y.; the front is black imprinted: "ACME SOAP"; lid is a replacement and the inside has been lined with old-timey calico patterned paper; held a hundred cakes, weight seventy-five pounds; 20″L x 15″W x 9″H.

SHIPPING BOX PANEL. Dovetailed and print still good; 19¼″L x 7″W. Products from wood boxes as this piece represents were sold right from the containers set on a counter or stores' floors. Make interesting wall hangings.

COLD DRINKS BOX. Pine; dated 1922; the inside and a separate inside lid are heavy rolled tin and retain the cold temperature; self-lift knob; iron latch holds inside lid firmly down; 44¼″W x 25½″D x 27¾″H. COCA COLA BOTTLE OPENER. Side-attached.

CANDY JARS. ca: 1800s. Each blown in a mold. One embossed: "Manufactured by HORNBY'S, Trade Mark U.S.Pat.Off. of BUTTERSCOTCH FAME"; applied top, bubbly aqua glass, no chips; glass lid fits into wide mouth with tiny dropoff; three pounds weight; pushed-up bottom and polished pontil.

One embossed: "ROBERT GIBSON & SONS LIMITED, LOZENGE MAKERS, MANCHESTER, ENGLAND"; same type lid as Hornby's; concaved base with tiny glass button pontil; three pounds weight; 13½″H x 4½″ dia.; both found at a former Florida Gulf Coast store.

SCALE SCOOPS. ca: 1800s. The larger is 11″L overall; uncommon back shaping of tins; red wood handles; smaller is 8¾″L.

CANDY TRAYS. ca: 1800s into early 1900s. Candy kitchens displayed their sweets, often made in a room back of their shops, on such pressed glass trays - these with a raised fan design on the back; 5¾″ x 7½″. CANDY SHELF POSTS. Candy shelves were often supported by these two-section fluted glass posts held by the screw-on silver-like bands; one part embossed "PATD."; posts reversible to use either end; various heights.

DERBY HAT MOLD. Hard maple; used by hatmaker; 5½" to 6¾" Dia.; Puritans wore high crowned wide brimmed beavers in contrast to the magnificently plumed big hats of the Cavaliers. Advancements reflected styles and materials suited to climates, fabrics at hand and personal preferences. The silk or beaver STOVEPIPES (great targets for snowballs) thru the 1700s into the 1800s (seen at pioneer developing settlements as well as in cities) were shunted into the background by the less cumbersome DERBY introduced in England by William Bowler.

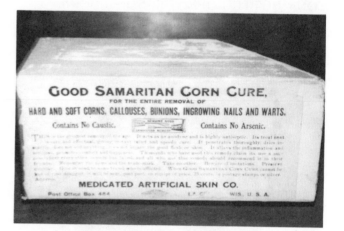

PATENT MAGNETO. Wooden box holds metal gears for two ratios, turned with the iron handle to activate; heavy rubber strips and a leather belt are broken; all original labels, printed: "A hand operated electric machine for self-induced shock, this for nervous disorders. Endorsed and used by the leading Physicians throughout United States and Europe". 4½"D x 10"W.

PAPER LABEL GOOD SAMARITAN CORN CURE by Medicated Artificial Skin Co. in Wisconsin, U.S.A. Typical of its era, this little panacea was also said to get rid of warts.

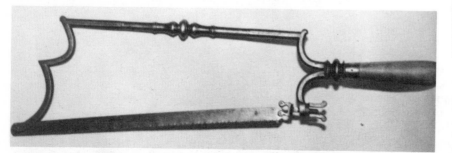

TIN BOXES MATERIA MEDICA. Glass top (peer-thru) tins from Parke Davis & Co. with scenics on all except bottom side; brass cotter pins hold lids; black on yellow; worn but readable; glass top uncommon.

SURGEON'S SAW. Brass and steel, wood handle; removable saw with one edge for cutting; an early tool elaborately designed.

GALLEY READY KEG. Very old; all wood with locked-lap wrapped hoops; fit-down-on-small-inside-ledge lid with self knob; stood beside ship's galley door ready for next mess (meal) preparation; Maine origin.

SHIP'S OFFICERS' TABLEWARE-CIVIL WAR USE. ca: 1860s. Still fairly well preserved, a 9″L bone-handled KNIFE, 7″L polished wood-handle FORK, and a silverplated SPOON, all brought up by divers after having been immersed for a hundred years on a blockade runner sunk during the latter days of the War off Fort Fisher, North Carolina, which guarded entry to the Wilmington Harbor. Framed to preserve.

BRONZE CANNONBALL. ca: War of 1812. Solidshot, soon replaced with iron since bronze was too expensive. Two part joined at center; 12 pounds weight; brought up from Lake Champlain after years of immersion. Said to have been "shot from" or "shot at" an American warship.

BOOM RINGS. ca: 1865-1900. Sails hauled down the halyards were rolled on the booms, rings then slipped over the furled sails holding them tightly, the beads making rolling easier; type once also used by smaller merchant ships.

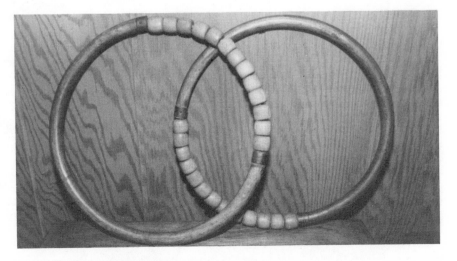

SHIP'S WHEEL. ca: 1700s. Canadian owner originally brought it here from West Germany where it's ship had navigated the Rhine River; teakwood with massive brass center fixture and ⅝"W brass inlay on both sides of 20½" dia. wheel, 27½" overall; eight wooden spokes.

SHIP'S WHEEL. ca: 1890. Six wood spokes grip; 36" dia. overall. ANCHOR LAMP. ca: 1800s. Blue glass chimney; brass and oil burner.

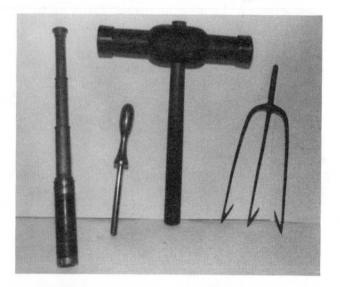

SHIP'S CAPT.'S TELESCOPE. ca: early 1800s. Scarce now to find in good condition; 16½"L open, 9" closed; smaller telescopes were called "Spyglasses." BELAYING PIN. Heavy brass, fit into side slots below ships' rails where ropes wrapped around were securely held (as pins and cleats are used); more often seen entirely of wood, or wood with leather; on old sailing vessels, etc. SHIP-WRIGHT'S CALKING HAMMER. For driving tarred oakum or twisted cotton-like wicking between seams in planks of wooden ships to help prevent leakage; iron collar/cups form wood mallet ends; four iron pins strengthened. FISH SPEAR. Wrought iron with original handle missing; 12"L as is.

SHIP'S WATER BOTTLE. ca: 1800s. From the Cunard Lines with original labels from many famous hotels. VERY heavy glass with a slight bluish tint; applied top glass ran down the sides in thick globs. (Rare).

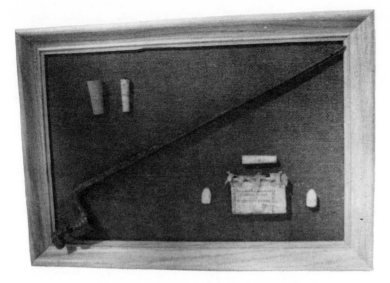

PINE FRAMED RELICS 1861-1865. About 20½"L overall BAYONET, three grooved sides with sharp point; during the Civil War, more were used to dig up vegetables in foraging, crush coffee beans in a cup, etc.; the socket end a candleholder, etc.

BOX of FUSES. Pasteboard type box with yellowed paper cover; ca: 1864 Frankford Arsenal; eight second FUSES.

INDIVIDUAL SMALL ARMS AMMUNITION and SEPARATE FUSES. 2"L paper spiral wrapped.

MINI SHOT. (Heavily reproduced).

SPONGE BUCKET. Civil War type; sheet iron; rivets held iron bail and links to fasten to artillery gun carriage axle; held water for dipping in a sponge on a long handle to wash out cannons. Today "Field Artillery Material" generally covers all related equipment, but to earlier artillerymen it meant only the wheeled vehicles as the cannons, limbers, caissons and so on. This is from a museum display.

Civil War. ca: 1861-65. BAYONET was bent in a lunge, striking an enemy's bone or the wielder slipping and hitting the point on the ground; three flat sides; socket top, very sharp point.

CAVALRY BRIDLE ROSETTES. Brass with floral center; half of a pair worn also on horse's bridle during western plains Indian Wars.

The smallest pair U.S. (Federal) BRIDLE ROSETTES.

ARTILLERY CANNON CLEANOUT PICK. Halfmoon brass grip, sharp pointed metal. (Issue to infantrymen for cleaning cone vents of their muskets were small pointed wires known as "Cone Pickers".)

SOLIDSHOT BALLS. Solid cast iron; this size principally anti-cavalry to unseat riders to infantry attack.

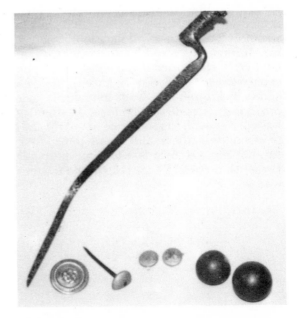

LOCKPLATE. ca: 1864. Framed later in pine; off a musket active in the Battle of Richmond, Virginia; spring-type top; 5¼" across, 3½"D.

PLUMB BOB. Iron; used by Civil War Engineers' Corps; attached to a plumb line it indicated a vertical position; also culd be a mariner's sounding line weight; "out of plumb" means "not a true line.".

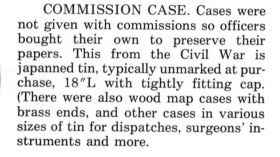

COMMISSION CASE. Cases were not given with commissions so officers bought their own to preserve their papers. This from the Civil War is japanned tin, typically unmarked at purchase, 18"L with tightly fitting cap. (There were also wood map cases with brass ends, and other cases in various sizes of tin for dispatches, surgeons' instruments and more.

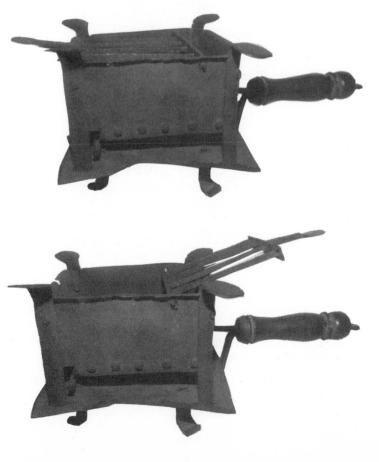

REVOLUTIONARY WAR CAMP STOVE. ca: 1775-1783. George Washington had these issued to his officers in the field; blacksmith-wrought iron with wood handle 6"L x 1½" dia.; ring for hanging on a tent pole when not being used; four 2"H whorled feet; almost a 6" square; live coals were scooped into the lower grille whose bar ends go through side walls horseshoe style, bent or mashed outside to hold firm; bars can be lifted for ash removal; the top grille bars held the teapot or such as skillets and small pans, four large thumbprint extensions affording more space for those; this RARITY also kept the owner mildly warm.

CLEAVER. Butcher's Tool of Spanish influence wrought iron and remains of brass over iron on the handle; whorled eye ring; found at the Civil War site of Fort Donelson, a Confederate fortification on the Cumberland River approach to Nashville, Tennessee; General Grant took the fort Feb. 12, 1862.

BLAKELY PROJECTILE. Civil War ARTILLERY SHOT about 7″ tall, 3¼″ dia.; CONFEDERATE STATES of AMERICA "spent" missile 4.3″ for Blakely cannon imported from England. (Rare).

CARTRIDGE BOX PLATE. Brass, shot damaged; found at a Civil War Depot near site of the Battle of Kennesaw, Georgia; 3⅛″ oval x 2⅛″W at center. These were used over and over on munitions boxes.

EAGLE BREAST STRAP MEDALLION. Federal infantrymen wore these at center on a wide leather strap going from the left shoulder across the chest to fasten at the right side of the waist belt, until it became too accurate a target for Southern sharpshooters; brass; 2½″ Dia.

BALL and CHAIN apparatus was used by both the Army and Navy, not, usually, for lesser offenses where prisoners were kept in permanent confinement areas at the rear, nor for lesser offenders who could be kept under armed guards, but for the serious offenders who must be kept closer to the front in more temporary quarters as guardhouses and compounds.

ANKLE (LEG) IRONS. These seen at a Museum as type used in the late 1700s and earlier 1800s; chain about 50″L.

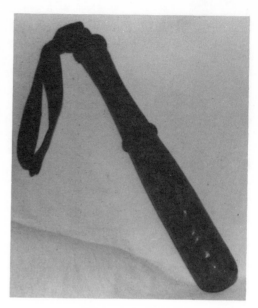

BILLY CLUB. ca: 1800s - early 1900s. Wood, partially leather wrapped and with strap for wrist toting, and swinging widely in walking; besides a weapon, police walking their "beats" banged the club hard and quickly against the curb stones and/or telephone poles, signalling information to officers in adjacent areas, the loud noise humming along the ground.

HANDCUFFS. ca: 1876. Used by Green County, Ohio law enforcement personnel; smithy-made; no key.

CARNIVAL MIRROR. Rarity; a thick brilliant glass beveled mirror has a large sunburst deeply cut at center on the underside facing front surface. Framed in honey maple with four wood rim balls, it reflected riders mounted on realistically carved and colorfully painted horses and other animals (with seats for those not wanting to ride up and down in saddled mounts on the iron poles) racing around and around on a merry-go-round. During the last of the 1800s into the earlier 1900s New Yorkers and other area city dwellers vacationed at Olcott, New York on Lake Ontario where the carnival owners of this mirror spent summer seasons in operation. There was a special thrill for all ages at hearing the blaring music, liberally accented with clashing cymbals, enticing customers; about 20″ across the middle.

CIRCUS POSTER. Printed paper now framed for preservation; M.L. Clark & Sons Shows; wonderfully typical 19th century entertainment; 28½″ x 11″.

PLAYBILL. ca: 1800s into early 1900s. A town's Opera House offered a variety of entertainments, (th' Oprey House usually upstairs over a store block) eagerly awaited far in advance, (early admissions 5¢). Traveling casts, with dogs and seals often along for animal acts, endured mediocre earnings in addition to stagecoach and/or train travel or both, smokey stench of lamps or lantern or candles as footlights, indifferent and uncertain meals, storms and other physical discomforts. All this to reap the enthusiastic applause at the close of their highly dramatic renditions. In raw areas, however, as mining camps, for instance, if displeased, the audience amid howls of derision might throw eggs and cabbages at the nimbly-dispersing actors. This thin paper stick-up Bill calls its presentation "The Greatest of the Railroad Plays"; about 8" x 4".

POLITICAL CAMPAIGN RIBBON. Originally worn as a badge. Fringed white silk with good readable black printing; framed on black velvet in a walnut shadowbox;
"For President HENRY CLAY, Vice-President T. Frelinghuysen; Governor Joseph Markle; Congress James Pollock; Mifflinburg Clay Club."
"Once more our glorious banner out upon the breeze we throw; Beneath its fold with song and shout Let's charge upon the foe."
He ran against James K. Polk in 1844. Tennessee origin.

## YESTERDAY ENRICHING TODAY

Whatever the reason for buying artifacts, to keep or for resale, condition is a large factor and how one deals with it. Hopefully, a light touch will correct structural weaknesses, while normal wear marks and fading finishes can be minimized without drastically changing the original appearance and intent of the maker. Buy what you will be able to live with. Do any necessary cleaning, set them out (if you still have space left) and enjoy them. Here are a few ideas others are using.

CHEESE HOOP. ca: 1800s. Wrapped wood, 11½" dia. x 6¾"H; effectively holds artificial red geraniums.

FUNNEL/STRAINER. Decorative on table as a candleholder in this position, lying on its side as a cornucopia with dried flowers, small fruits, herbs and/or wrapped candies spilling out or simply hung on a wall.

ORANGE CRATES (SHIPPING BOXES) SHELVES. Shop display applicable in homes for favorite collectibles or books; these have two sections wood divided, those and end tops are metal covered. Boxes of other products could be used.

COFFEE CATCHER. Roasted coffee beans were poured into the top hopper of a large machine, crushed or ground by inside gears, and dropped through a funnel-type tube into this catcher's top mouth; the coffee then was usually poured through the one-side round spout into, usually, one to five-pound sacks for store customers. The wide flat handle has a center roll to facilitate handling. All original with red japanned finish, black striping and a small gilt flower on each side; 8¾"H without top guard; 14"L without handle; 6½"W. Especially attractive for dried flower arrangements in a country kitchen. A few catchers have been seen in green.

COFFEE POT. Gray GRANITE-WARE with attached tin lid having wood knob; the handle's wide middle makes for better pouring control; lapped seams. 6½"H x 5½" dia. base.

CANDLE BOX. Hand-made copper for wall hanging; while driving in a far western state, friends stopped at a wayside stand and noticed this nailed to the side of the barn. With no antique or sentimental significance to the farm-inheritors, they readily sold it. The elbow grease and cleaners it demanded was more than compensated by its final gleam.

MILL SPOOLS. ca: 1800s. The earlier style, New Hampshire origin. Wood with small grooved circles below the straight-edge tops. Attractive alone, in pairs, or in candleholder groupings.

TOOL CHEST. ca: 1800s. Chestnut; four sides dovetailed; pine panels; 37″L x 22¼″W x 22″H. Now a family room fireside table.

MILL SPOOLS. (Now practical Candlesticks). Heights and diameters vary greatly according to required use at mills, winding thread, for one; these from a Georgia cotton mill, are dogwood with metal bound top and bottom circles; 6½″ to 12½″H.

PRINTER'S TYPESET TRAY. Wood with metal pull; today miniatures fit nicely into slots; made in various sizes.

LAUNDRY BOX. ca: 1800s. When a Pennsylvania Amish man needed a stand for the walnut clothes box he'd made for his wife, he used the one which also could hold her washboiler and tubs (could be folded for storage when not in use).

HALL VIEW. Children's Oldies, a STAKEWAGON.

MAPLE TABLE.

Loopback KITCHEN WINDSOR CHAIRS of mixed woods.

MILL SPOOL CANDLE HOLDER. Miscellaneous articles added for decoration.

Collection of CANDLE HOLDERS. ca: 1700s and 1800s. Brass in various sizes.

Glass CANDY SHELF HOLDERS. (While unrelated, the center alabaster carving and other miscellany fit in nicely, as does the new mirror; hand-cut from old tin to represent Pennsylvania Dutch work.).

FARM WALL INTEREST. CAR-
RIAGE WHEEL, leather HORSE COL-
LAR, iron HAMES with brass tops; ideal for
a business complex or at home; the wheel's
axle and binding on the outer edge of the
wooden wheels are iron.

SLED.          ca:
1800s. Hickory, all
original; upended in a
narrow hall with a
board laid across for
a shelf, furnishing a
novel spot for a
DOLLS' TRUNK.

SLED. ca: 1800s. Makes a novel
and useful low chairside table.

Seen in a Tennessee kitchen. CAN-
DY MOLDS and a shelf made by hanging an ancient wooden ORGAN NOTE.

LOBSTER TRAP. Slats construction with fishnet snares, and a new glass top added to convert it into an unusual low table; 35″L x 19″W x 14″H.

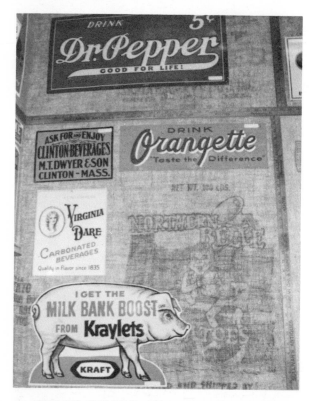

WALL DECOR. For a small open office area of his shop, a dealer bought old (and not so old) burlap bags originally holding grain, potatoes, etc., had them carefully professionally laundered and pressed, ripped the seams, and with adhesives covered the walls. Yard sticks covered the edges, framing each sack. (The signs were for sale: DR. PEPPER ca: late 1920s-1930s; ORANGETTE ca: 1957; CLINTON ca: 1930; VIRGINIA DARE ca: 1950s; KRAYLETS PIG ca: 1950.

TABLE LEGS HANGERS. ca: 1800s. Tired of moving aside this wood stashed in a shed on his farm, (and not having any spare table board tops), one dealer offered these at a Nashville, Tennessee show. The added square nails can hold candles in pairs with uncut wicks, towels, knickknacks, etc. One is original finish solid walnut, two have patches of blue and red, white and blue original paint, the paint increasing their appeal.

ORNAMENTAL BRASS PANEL. Hand-hammered convex laurel-crowned head with toga-draped shoulders on a 14″ x 18″ panel. Tin was more often used as ceilings in old stores, brass and copper in courthouses, etc.; 22½″H x 18″W.

PART FROM A MILKING MACHINE decorative in an office or home foyer. Thin tin coating worn in spots from the heavy copper; "DELAVAL" impressed on plates below each ear; only the locking-handle-top and the bail are iron; (beautiful if the old tin is removed by reverse-electrolysis); wt. 15⅞ pounda, 19″ tall without bail, 12″ dia. base slightly wider at its bulbous middle. Seen in Wisconsin.

DISPLAY STAND. Yellow metal with red advertising for Royal Crown Cola which is practical in a home for collectibles; fits nicely into a corner.

TABLE. ca: 1800s. First an original big butterworker; then with its heavy wood roller that fit into a hole at the shorter legged end obsolete, according to fading pictures it served a second purpose. Women in old style shoe-length dresses and sunbonnets standing on each table side were seen busily sorting cranberries. And at long last the Butterworker/Cranberry Sorter has become an interesting furniture piece in a home. If the present owner wanted it leveled, that would be a simple matter and not destroy its overall original appearance.

# Value Guide

N.P.A. - No prices available.

**Page 7**
Cornsheller, rare . . . . . . . . . . . . . $195.00
**Page 8**
Wood Measures, 8″ dia. . . . . . . $125.00
    6¾″ dia. . . . . . . . . . . . . . . . $125.00
    5¾″ dia. . . . . . . . . . . . . . . . $100.00
Grain Measure . . . . . . . . . . . . . . . $85.00
Measures . . . . . . . . . . . . $55.00-145.00
**Page 9**
Grain Measure . . . . . . . . . . . . . . . $75.00
Grain Measure . . . . . . . . . . . . . . . $95.00
Seed Grains Scraper . . . . . . . . . . $12.50
Seedcorn Dryers . . . . . . . . each $18.00
**Page 10**
Steelyards . . . . . . . . . . . . . . . . . . $75.00
**Page 11**
Buhr (Grinding) Stone . . . . . . . . . N.P.A.
Meal Scoop (Palette) . . . . . . . . . . $28.00
Gristmill Hand Grinder . . . . . . . . . N.P.A.
**Page 12**
Grain Shovel . . . . . . . . . . . . . . . . $175.00
Grain Scoop . . . . . . . . . . . . . . . . $135.00
Grains Scraper (Puller) . . . . . . . . $40.00
**Page 13**
Seed Measure . . . . . . . . . . . . . . . $18.00
Towsack Needle . . . . . . . . . . . . . . $6.00
Sign . . . . . . . . . . . . . . . . . . . . . . $350.00+
**Page 14**
Lard Squeezer . . . . . . . . . . . . . . . $55.00
Sausage Gun . . . . . . . . . . . . . . . . $65.00
**Page 15**
Axe Head . . . . . . . . . . . . . . . . . . . $75.00
American Goosewing Broadaxe . $225.00
Hitting Maul (Beetle) . . . . . . . . . . $28.00
**Page 16**
Loggers' Pickaroon . . . . . . . . . . . $29.00
Mallet . . . . . . . . . . . . . . . . . . . . . . $32.50
Knife Frow . . . . . . . . . . . . . . . . . $150.00
Silage Cutter . . . . . . . . . . . . . . . . $45.00
Well Plug . . . . . . . . . . . . . . . . . . . $22.50
**Page 17**
Chuckwagon Pail . . . . . . . . . . . . . $25.00
Well Bucket . . . . . . . . . . . . . . . . . $25.00
Leather Bucket . . . . . . . . . . . . . . $125.00
Wheelbarrow Wheel . . . . . . . . . . . $20.00
**Page 18**
Grubbing Hoe . . . . . . . . . . . . . . . $50.00
Cabbage Planter . . . . . . . . . . . . . $35.00
Gig . . . . . . . . . . . . . . . . . . . . . . . . $65.00
Bluegrass Seed Stripper . . . . . . $125.00
Cranberry Scoop . . . . . . . . . . . . $125.00
**Page 19**
Grape Picker's Hamper (Basket) $275.00
Wine Barrel Stopper . . . . . . . . . . $18.00
Wool Combs, right . . . . . . . . . . . $135.00
    left . . . . . . . . . . . . . . . . . . . . $185.00+
**Page 20**
Flax Swingle . . . . . . . . . . . . . . . . $175.00
Wool Carders . . . . . . . . . . . pair $38.00
**Page 21**
Flax Knife . . . . . . . . . . . . . . . . . . $145.00
Fruit Press . . . . . . . . . . . . . . . . . $275.00
**Page 22**
Honey Press . . . . . . . . . . . . . . . . $350.00+
Beehive Box . . . . . . . . . . . . . . . . $125.00
Queen Bee Box . . . . . . . . . . . . . . $45.00
**Page 23**
Sorghum Stalk Grinder . . . . . . . . N.P.A.
**Page 24**
Field Knife . . . . . . . . . . . . . . . . . . $18.00
Stalk (Fodder) Leaf Stripper . . . . $22.50
Cane Stalk Leaf Stripper . . . . . . $25.00
Covered Wagon Trunk/Box . . . . $295.00
Braking (Drag) Shoe . . . . . . . . . . $38.00

**Page 25**
Grab for Snatch Team . . . . . . . . . $45.00
Grease Bucket, left . . . . . . . . . . . $85.00
Grease Bucket, right . . . . . . . . . . $45.00
**Page 26**
Draghook . . . . . . . . . . . . . . . . . . . $22.50
Chain . . . . . . . . . . . . . . . . . . . . . . $22.50
Wagon Hammer . . . . . . . . . . . . . . $25.00
Wagon Keg . . . . . . . . . . . . . . . . . $100.00
Wagon Jacks, 30″ . . . . . . . . . . . . $55.00
    26″ . . . . . . . . . . . . . . . . . . . . . $35.00
**Page 27**
Wagon Tool Box . . . . . . . . . . . . . $45.00
Comb . . . . . . . . . . . . . . . . . . . . . . $25.00
Animal Bell . . . . . . . . . . . . . . . . . $145.00
**Page 28**
Shoes . . . . . . . . . . . . . each $8.00-28.00
Bits . . . . . . . . . . . . . . . . $10.00-35.00
Uncommon Mule Collar . . . . . . . $45.00
Horsecollar . . . . . . . . . . . . . . . . . $45.00
Harness Hooks, large . . . . . . . . . $40.00
    small . . . . . . . . . . . . each $35.00
**Page 29**
Harness Horse (Stitcher) . . . . . . $175.00
Unusual Harness Horse . . . . . . . $225.00
Harness Yoke . . . . . . . . . . . . . . . $45.00
Horse Anchor (Hitching Weight) . $25.00
**Page 30**
Hitching Weight (Tether) . . . . . . . $22.50
Goat Yoke . . . . . . . . . . . . . . . . . . $75.00
Goat Collar and Singletree . . set $75.00
Calf's Yoke with Poke . . . . . . . . . $22.50
**Page 31**
Calf Muzzle . . . . . . . . . . . . . . . . . $35.00
Calf Muzzle . . . . . . . . . . . . . . . . . $18.00
Workhorse Shoe . . . . . . . . . . . . . $10.00
Calves' Saltbox . . . . . . . . . . . . . . $35.00
Farm Fork . . . . . . . . . . . . . . . . . . $55.00
**Page 32**
Dehorning Shears . . . . . . . . . . . . $40.00
"WC" Branding Iron . . . . . . . . . . $38.00
"RC" Branding Iron . . . . . . . . . . $28.00
Elephant Head Branding Iron . . . $45.00
**Page 33**
Ginseng Hoe . . . . . . . . . . . . . . . . $40.00
Tanner's Unhairing Knife . . . . . . $55.00
Brick Mold, 5¾″W . . . . . . $85.00-125.00
Brick Mold, 3¾″W . . . . . . $65.00-75.00
**Page 34**
Rare Brick . . . . . . . . . . . . . . . . . . $75.00
**Page 35**
Bricks . . . . . . . . . . . . . . each $12.50
Brick . . . . . . . . . . . . . . . . . . . . . . $28.00
Small Tool Box . . . . . . . . . . . . . . $125.00
Tool Carrier . . . . . . . . . . . . . . . . . $85.00
**Page 36**
Tool Carrier . . . . . . . . . . . . . . . . $125.00
Shaving Horses, top . . . . . . . . . $175.00
    bottom . . . . . . . . . . . . . . . . $150.00
**Page 37**
Whiskey Still "Thieves" . . . each $22.50
Whiskey Still Masher . . . . . . . . . $25.00
Hammer (Mallet) . . . . . . . . . . . . . $40.00
Wheelwright's Reamer . . . . . . . . $75.00
**Page 38**
Special Purpose Anvil . . . . . . . . $100.00
Mantrap . . . . . . . . . . . . . . . . . . . $250.00+
Primitive Canada Goose . . . . . . $275.00
**Page 39**
Canada Goose Decoy (Marsh) . $125.00
Canada Goose Decoy, 21″L . . . $275.00
Canada Goose Decoy, 28″L . . . $325.00
Sleeper (Confidence Duck Decoy) $125.00

**Page 40**
Canada Goose Decoy . . . . . . . . . $350.00
Bufflehead Duck Decoy
    (Buffalohead) . . . . . . . . . . . $95.00
Maine Goose Decoy . . . . . . . . . . $55.00
Canada Goose Decoy, Sleeper
    and Watcher . . . . . . . . . set $250.00
**Page 41**
Confidence Duck Decoy . . . . . . . $150.00
Mallard Hen Decoy . . . . . . . . . . $195.00
Woodduck Decoy . . . . . . . . . . . $195.00
Mallard Hen Decoy . . . . . . . . . . $200.00
Mallard Male Decoy . . . . . . . . . . $185.00
**Page 42**
Primitive Duck Decoy . . . . . . . . . $95.00
Canvasback Duck Decoy . . . . . . $250.00
New Canada Goose Decoy . . . . . $375.00
New Pintail Hen Decoy . . . . . . . . $35.00
New Pintail Drake Decoy . . . . . . $35.00
**Page 43**
Umbilical Cord Bag
    (Gila Monster) . . . . . . . $175.00-250.00
Basket . . . . . . . . . . . . . . $125.00-150.00
Trade Axe . . . . . . . . . . . $100.00-150.00
Pipe Tamper . . . . . . . . . $125.00-175.00
Pipe Cleaner . . . . . . . . . $100.00-150.00
Pottery Vessels . . . . . . . $125.00-175.00
Pottery Shallow Bowl . . . $125.00-165.00
**Page 44**
Andirons (Firedogs) . . . . . pair $200.00+
Skillet . . . . . . . . . . . . . . . . . . . . . $175.00
Andirons . . . . . . . . . . . . . pair $150.00
Other Items . . . . . . . . . . . . . . . . . N.P.A.
**Page 45**
Fireplace Swinging Crane . . . . . . $175.00
Fireplace Crane . . . . . . . . . . . . . . $75.00
Skewer Rest, rare . . . . . . . . . . . . $300.00
Utensil and Light Game Board . $275.00
**Page 46**
Double Pothooks . . . . . . . . . . . . . $95.00
Handforging, Part of Hanger . . . . $5.00
Grappling Hook . . . . . . . . . . . . . . $55.00
Trammel Hook . . . . . . . . . . . . . . . $42.50
**Page 47**
Fireplace Ash Shovels, Pokers
    and Flue Rakes . . . . . . . $7.50-35.00
Fireplace Pokers . . . . . . . . each $28.00
**Page 48**
Hearth Grille . . . . . . . . . . . . . . . . $285.00+
Hearth Toaster . . . . . . . . . . . . . . $285.00+
Trivet . . . . . . . . . . . . . . . $75.00-125.00
Trivets, 6½″ dia. . . . . . . . . . . . . . $25.00
    Footman . . . . . . . . . . $95.00-125.00
**Page 49**
Splinters Box, rare . . . . . . . . . . . $150.00
Bootscraper . . . . . . . . . . . . . . . . . $175.00
Oven Peel . . . . . . . . . . . . . . . . . . $40.00
Chestnut Roaster . . . . . . . . . . . . $195.00
Cotton Grain Bag . . . . . . . . . . . . $15.00
**Page 50**
Milk Pails . . . . . . . . . . each $35.00-40.00
Water Buckets . . . . . . . . . each $100.00+
**Page 51**
Tub . . . . . . . . . . . . . . . . . . . . . . . $100.00+
Butter Churn (Dasher) . . . . . . . . $165.00
Rocking Butter Churn . . . . . . . . . $375.00
Butter Churn . . . . . . . . . . . . . . . . $350.00
**Page 52**
Keeler . . . . . . . . . . . . . . . . . . . . . $150.00
Butterworker (Scoop) . . . . . . . . . $75.00
**Page 53**
Butter Carriers . . . . . each $175.00-185.00
**Page 54**
Butter Mold . . . . . . . . . . . . . . . . . $175.00

Butter Mold and Worker
  (Paddle), similar . . . . . . . . . set $250.00
Cheese Mixing Bowl . . . . . . . . . $135.00
Curds Knife . . . . . . . . . . . . . . . . . $75.00
Cheese Curd Breaker . . . . . . . . . $225.00

**Page 55**
Cheese Keeper . . . . . . . . . . . . . . . $95.00
Cheese Drainer with Ladder . . . . $550.00
Cheese Dish (Keeper) . . . . . . . . . $295.00
Cheese Drainer . . . . . . . . . . . . . . $110.00

**Page 56**
Cheese Cutter . . . . . . . . . . . . . . . $95.00
Lidded Pantry Box . . . . . . . . . . . $65.00
Cheese Hoop . . . . . . . . . . . . . . . . $75.00
Egg Weigher . . . . . . . . . . . . . . . . $22.50
Hen's Egg . . . . . . . . . . . . . . . . . . . $6.00
Duck or Goose Eggs . . . . . $10.00-15.00

**Page 57**
Egg Sorter . . . . . . . . . . . . . . . . . $175.00
Apple Parer . . . . . . . . . . . . . . . . $245.00
Burl Bowl . . . . . . . . . . . . . . . . . . $225.00
Apple Drying Rack . . . . . . . . . . $150.00
Applebutter Paddle . . . . . . . . . . . $95.00

**Page 58**
Yard Kettle, top . . . . . . . . . . . . . $395.00
Yard Kettle, bottom . . . . . . . . . . $550.00
Nutmeg Grater . . . . . . . . . . . . . . $75.00

**Page 59**
Dipper . . . . . . . . . . . . . . . . . . . . . $85.00
Eating Tray (Bowl, Dish) . . . . . . $195.00
Doughraiser (Bowl) . . . . . . . . . . $135.00

**Page 60**
Doughtray (Mixer, Bowl) . . . . . . $225.00
Doughraiser . . . . . . . . . . . . . . . . $225.00
Rolling Pins, large . . . . . . . . . . . $65.00
  16"-18" . . . . . . . . . . . $45.00-55.00
  15½" . . . . . . . . . . . . . . . . . . . $55.00
  12" . . . . . . . . . . . . . . . . . . . . $35.00

**Page 61**
Shaker Dough Roller Set, rare . . $195.00
Dough (Pastry) Board . . . . . . . . . $65.00
Dough Box Rolling Board . . . . . . $60.00

**Page 62**
Strainer-Funnel . . . . . . . . . . . . . $35.00
Food Paddles . . . . . . . . . . each $35.00
Cabbage Cutter (Slicer) . . . . . . . $125.00
Food Paddle . . . . . . . . . . . . . . . . $35.00
Kraut Weight . . . . . . . . . . . . . . . . $5.00

**Page 63**
Food Knives (Choppers) . . . each $95.00
Chopping Knives . . . each $55.00-100.00

**Page 64**
Iron Skimmer . . . . . . . . . . . . . . . $65.00
Dipper . . . . . . . . . . . . . . . . . . . . . $65.00
Fork . . . . . . . . . . . . . . . . . . . . . . . $65.00
Pastry Mold . . . . . . . . . . . . . . . . $160.00
Flour Barrel . . . . . . . . . . . . . . . . . $45.00
Sugar Grinder . . . . . . . . . . . . . . $125.00
Tankard . . . . . . . . . . . . . . . . . . . $225.00
Flour Sifter . . . . . . . . . . . . . . . . $185.00
Cheesekeeper . . . . . . . . . . . . . . . $95.00

**Page 65**
Polished Nippers . . . . . . . . . . . $150.00+
Maple Sugar Molds . each $75.00-225.00
Molds Set . . . . . . . . . . . . . . . . . . $45.00
Candy Molds . . . . . . each $25.00-35.00

**Page 66**
Mold . . . . . . . . . . . . . . . . . . . . . . $45.00
Divided Roaster . . . . . . . . . . . . . $40.00
Cup . . . . . . . . . . . . . . . . . . . . . . . $17.50
Funnel . . . . . . . . . . . . . . . . . . . . . $18.00
Posnet . . . . . . . . . . . . . . . . . . . . . $90.00

**Page 67**
Tumblers . . . . . . . . . . . . each $7.50
Lunch Pail . . . . . . . . . . . . . . . . . . $75.00
Chuckwagon Pan . . . . . . . . . . . . $35.00
Tin Funnel, large . . . . . . . . . . . . . $8.50
Tin Funnel, small . . . . . . . . . . . . . $7.50
Scrapple Pan . . . . . . . . . . . . . . . . $65.00

Dishpan . . . . . . . . . . . . . . . . . . . $35.00
**Page 68**
Open Roaster . . . . . . . . . . . . . . . $40.00
Redware Jar . . . . . . . . . . . . . . . . $75.00
Slipware Pitcher . . . . . . . . . . . . . $125.00
Slipware Plate . . . . . . . . . . . . . . . $95.00
Redware Mold . . . . . . . . . . . . . . $95.00
Redware Pie Plate . . . . . . . . . . . $95.00
Yellowware Pie Plate . . . . . . . . . $68.00
Yellowware Pie Plate . . . . . . . . . $75.00

**Page 69**
Yellowware . . . . . . . . . . . . . . . . . $65.00
Pudding Bowl . . . . . . . . . . . . . . . $45.00
Stoneware Crock, 9½"H . . . . . . $300.00
Stoneware Crock, 7¼"H . . . . . . . $45.00
Chop Plate . . . . . . . . . . . . . . . . . $35.00

**Page 70**
Stoneware Jug . . . . . . . . . . . . . . $225.00
Stoneware Jugs, large . . . . . . . . . $95.00
  small . . . . . . . . . . . . . . . . . . . $85.00
Mold, Graniteware . . . . . . . . . . . $75.00
Tin Cup . . . . . . . . . . . . . . . . . . . . $10.00
Candlestick . . . . . . . . . . . . . . . . . $35.00
Little Bucket . . . . . . . . . . . . . . . . $22.50

**Page 71**
Graniteware Pitcher . . . . . . . . . . $65.00
Doorstop (Door Porter) . . . . . . . . $75.00
Household Mortars and
  Pestles, left . . . . . . . . . . . . . . $175.00
  right . . . . . . . . . . . . . . . . . . . $195.00

**Page 72**
Lap Coffee Grinder . . . . . . . . . . . $75.00
Coffee Grinder . . . . . . . . . . . . . . $85.00
Wall Hanging Coffee Grinder . . . . $55.00
Cast Iron Trivets . . . each $15.00-18.00
Coffee Pot (Server) . . . . . . . . . . . $250.00

**Page 73**
Teakettle . . . . . . . . . . . . . . . . . . . $95.00
Saucepan . . . . . . . . . . . . . . . . . . $110.00
Paperweight . . . . . . . . . . . . . . . . $25.00
Broom Holder . . . . . . . . . . . . . . . $18.00
Quilt . . . . . . . . . . . . . . . . . . . . . . $350.00

**Page 74**
Scrubber (Scouring) Boxes . each $95.00
Pillow Fluffers, Heart Centers . . . $25.00
  Heavier Wire . . . . . . . . . . . . . $22.50
Lye Soap Cutter . . . . . . . . . . . . . $75.00

**Page 75**
Carpet Beaters . . . . . . . $25.00-75.00
Shaker Carpet Beater . . . . . . . . . $75.00
Pose' Stick (Dolly Peg) . . . . . . . . $40.00

**Page 76**
Washing Peg . . . . . . . . . . . . . . . . $35.00
Dolly Pegs . . . . . . . . . . . each $125.00

**Page 77**
Washstick . . . . . . . . . . . . . . . . . . $45.00
Scrub (Wash) Board . . . . . . . . . . $55.00

**Page 78**
Scrub Boards, left . . . . . . . . . . . $75.00
  middle . . . . . . . . . . . . . . . . . . $38.00
  right . . . . . . . . . . . . . . . . . . . . $55.00
Washboiler . . . . . . . . . . . . . . . . $150.00+

**Page 79**
Sadirons (Laundry), small . . . . . $25.00
  everyday . . . . . . . . . . . . . . . . $22.50
Ironing Board . . . . . . . . . . . . . . . $45.00

**Page 80**
Stocking and Sock Forms . . pair $38.00
  rare oversize . . . . . . . . . . . . . $40.00
Shapers and Dryers . . each $22.00-28.00
Coal Saver . . . . . . . . . . . . . . . . . $65.00

**Page 81**
Kerosene Stove Reservoirs . each $35.00
Flowers Gathering Basket . . . . . . $115.00
Market Basket . . . . . . . . . . . . . . $95.00
Garden Basket . . . . . . . . . . . . . $175.00+
Egg (Utility) Basket . . . . . . . . . . $200.00

**Page 82**
Gathering Basket . . . . . . . . . . . . $150.00

Oval Basket . . . . . . . . . . . . . . . . $165.00
Rye Straw Basket . . . . . . . . . . . . $200.00
Buttocks Basket . . . . . . . . . . . . . $150.00
Decorative Basket . . . . . . . . . . . . $90.00
Table Basket . . . . . . . . . . . . . . . . $45.00

**Page 83**
Pantry/Table Basket . . . . . . . . . . $145.00
Table Basket . . . . . . . . . . . . . . . . $75.00
Basket Carrier . . . . . . . . . . . . . . . $38.00
Apple Basket . . . . . . . . . . . . . . . $175.00

**Page 84**
Field Basket . . . . . . . . . . . . . . . . $200.00
Fishing Basket . . . . . . . . . . . . . . $58.00
Miniature (Lunch) Picnic Basket $125.00+
Wire Field Basket . . . . . . . . . . . . $45.00

**Page 85**
Wire Store Baskets . . each $35.00-40.00
"Go Cart" Basket . . . . . . . . . . . . $295.00
Schoolgirl Art Box . . . . . . . . . . . $200.00
Box . . . . . . . . . . . . . . . . . . . . . . . $275.00
Ballot Box . . . . . . . . . . . . . . . . . . $47.50

**Page 86**
"Till" Box . . . . . . . . . . . . . . . . . . $150.00
Shipping Box . . . . . . . . . . . . . . . $150.00
Desk/Counter Box . . . . . . . . . . . $42.50
Silver Box . . . . . . . . . . . . . . . . . . $175.00

**Page 87**
Travel Trunk . . . . . . . . . . . . . . . . $95.00
Cowhide Trunk . . . . . . . . . . . . . . $145.00

**Page 88**
Travel Box . . . . . . . . . . . . . . . . . $195.00
Trunk . . . . . . . . . . . . . . . . . . . . . $125.00
Candlemolds, 11" . . . . . . . . . . . $110.00
  10½" . . . . . . . . . . . . . . . . . . $125.00
Candle Drying Rack . . . . . . . . . . $75.00

**Page 89**
Candle Box . . . . . . . . . . . . . . . . . $165.00
Candleholders . . . . . . . . . . pair $250.00
Push-up Candlesticks . . . . . pair $250.00
Candlespikes . . . . . . each $150.00-195.00

**Page 90**
Miners' Candlespikes each $100.00-125.00
Smaller Candlespike . . . . . $85.00-100.00
Wall Lamp . . . . . . . . . . . . . . . . . $40.00
Candleholder . . . . . . . . . . . . . . . . $18.00
Hogscraper Candleholder . . . . . . $95.00
Tin Lamps . . . . . . . . . . $125.00-375.00
Candlemolds . . . . . . . . . $175.00-275.00

**Page 91**
Hanging Lamp . . . . . . . . . . . . . $395.00+
Hanging Lamp (Lantern) . . . . . . $45.00
Fishing Lamp (Lantern) . . . . . . . $115.00
Hanging Lamp . . . . . . . . . . . . . . $95.00

**Page 92**
Wall Lamp . . . . . . . . . . . . . . . . . $125.00
Miniature Hand Lamps . $195.00-250.00
Camphene Lamp . . . . . . . . . . . . $325.00
Kettle Lamp . . . . . . . . . . . . . . . . $275.00

**Page 93**
Miniature Lamps . . . . . . . . . . . . $185.00
Unusual Miniature . . . . . . . . . . . $185.00
Lacemaker's or Dressmaker's
  Lamp . . . . . . . . . . . . . . . . . . $395.00
Brooder Lamps . . . . . each $35.00-40.00

**Page 94**
Bench . . . . . . . . . . . . . . . . . . . . . $235.00
Cotton Bag . . . . . . . . . . . . . . . . . $12.50
Bench, 10"H . . . . . . . . . . . . . . . $115.00
Bench, 16½"H . . . . . . . . . . . . . $185.00
Bench, 16"H . . . . . . . . . . . . . . . $125.00

**Page 95**
Deacon's Bench . . . . . . . . . . . . . $425.00
Mammy Bench . . . . . . . . . . . . $1,200.00+
Grain Bin . . . . . . . . . . . . . . . . . . $195.00
Meal Bin . . . . . . . . . . . . . . . . . . $450.00+

**Page 96**
Meal and Flour Bin . . . . . . . . . . $475.00
Meal Bin . . . . . . . . . . . . . . . . . . $850.00+
Meal Bin . . . . . . . . . . . . . . . . . . $225.00

# Cover Items:

Cover items courtesy of Chris Blackburn and Kay B. Smith.

# Two Important Tools For The
## Astute Antique Dealer, Collector and Investor

## Schroeder's Antiques Price Guide

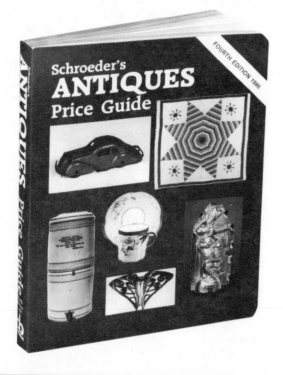

The very best low cost investment that you can make if you are really serious about antiques and collectibles is a good identification and price guide. We publish and highly recommend **Schroeder's Antiques Price Guide.** Our editors and writers are very careful to seek out and report accurate values each year. We do not simply change the values of the items each year but start anew to bring you an entirely new edition. If there are repeats, they are by chance and not by choice. Each huge edition (it weighs 3 pounds!) has over 50,000 descriptions and current values on 608 - 8½x11 pages. There are hundreds and hundreds of categories and even more illustrations. Each topic is introduced by an interesting discussion that is an education in itself. Again, no dealer, collector or investor can afford not to own this book. It is available from your favorite bookseller or antiques dealer at the low price of $11.95. If you are unable to find this price guide in your area, it's available from Collector Books, P.O. Box 3009, Paducah, KY 42001 at $11.95 plus $1.00 for postage and handling.

## Flea Market Trader

Bargains are pretty hard to come by these days -- especially in the field of antiques and collectibles, and everyone knows that the most promising sources for those seldom-found under-priced treasures are flea markets. To help you recognize a bargain when you find it, you'll want a copy of the *Flea Market Trader*--the only price guide on the market that deals exclusively with all types of merchandise you'll be likely to encounter in the marketplace. It contains not only reliable pricing information, but the *Flea Market Trader* will be the first to tune you in to the market's newest collectible interests -- you will be able to buy before the market becomes established, before prices have a chance to escalate! You'll not only have the satisfaction of being first in the know, but you'll see your investments appreciate dramatically. You will love the format. Its handy 5½"x8½" size will tuck easily into pocket or purse. Its common sense organization along with detailed index makes finding your subject a breeze. There's tons of information and hundreds of photos to aid in identification. It's written with first-hand insight and an understanding of market activities. It's reliable, informative, comprehensive; it's a bargain! From Collector Books, P.O. Box 3009 Paducah, Kentucky 42001. $8.95 plus $1.00 postage and handling.